HOW A MAN
TAKES CARE OF HIMSELF

LifeSkills for Men

Also of Interest

9710

LIFESKILLS
FOR MEN

HOW A MAN
TAKES
CARE OF
HIMSELF

JIM HALL

DAVID HAZARD, *General Editor*

BETHANY HOUSE PUBLISHERS
MINNEAPOLIS, MINNESOTA 55438

Published by Bethany House Publishers
A Ministry of Bethany Fellowship International
11300 Hampshire Avenue South
Minneapolis, Minnesota 55438

Printed in the United States of America by
Bethany Press International, Minneapolis, Minnesota 55438

Library of Congress Cataloging-in-Publication Data

Hall, James, 1953–
    How a man takes care of himself / by James Hall.
        p. cm. — (Lifeskills for men)
    ISBN 1–55661–678–3 pbk.
    1. Men—Religious life. 2. Men—Life skills guide.
3. Christian life. I. Title. II. Series.
BV4528.2.H34   1998
248.8'42—ddc21   97–45438
                                                          CIP

To my wife and my son,
and to Christian friends,
who make THIS man know
that he is loved
and that he is blessed!

JAMES HALL is an award-winning, free-lance writer and former newspaper editor and reporter. He is an ordained pastor and has a biblically based natural health and nutrition counseling ministry. Hall has college degrees in both journalism and nutrition. His wife, Mary, is a special education teacher in Indianapolis, and the couple has one son, Lincoln. They reside in Shelbyville, Indiana.

Acknowledgments

This project had its genesis in a handwritten letter I wrote many months ago at two in the morning.

My toddler son had been sick and I'd stayed up with him until he fell asleep. Unable to sleep myself, I went looking for something to read and found a copy of *Charisma* magazine.

Flipping through its pages, I happened upon a piece written by David Hazard. Since I'd communicated with David in the past as one Christian writer to another, I was pleased to see that he'd begun doing a regular column for *Charisma*.

In this particular issue of the magazine, David recounted a time of serious illness in his life and explained how God had brought him through that ordeal. Boy, could I relate! Like David, I'd also recently been through a time of struggling with health problems.

I wrote a letter to David in the wee hours of that morning, telling him how much I'd appreciated the article and filling him in on some of the details of my life since we'd last communicated. A couple of weeks later, I received a letter back from him. In it, David mentioned that he was editing a series of books for Christian men and wondered if I'd have any interest in doing a book instructing men about how to take care of themselves.

I think my heart must have skipped two or three beats! I'd been looking for an opportunity to do precisely what David was suggesting in his letter. I wanted to use the written word to help instruct others so that they wouldn't have to endure anything like what David and I had been through. My prayers were being answered.

Thank you, David Hazard, for many things. Thanks for your confidence in me and for your ongoing support, encouragement, and expertise as an editor.

I'd also like to thank the hardest-working woman in America. Mary, my wife of eighteen years, should get a medal of honor just for putting up with me for close to two decades. Instead, I gave her the job of being my first-line copy editor for this project.

Mary's a woman who, along with taking good care of her family and being my copy editor, commutes every weekday to teach special education in an inner-city elementary school. She also makes the best vegetarian lasagna on the face of this planet. Mary, where would I be without you? Don't answer that!

Finally, thanks to Bethany House Publishers for caring enough about Christian men to publish this very important LifeSkills book series.

————

fessional. The reader should consult with his personal physician before taking any food supplement or herbal product mentioned in this book and before initiating any exercise program.

Contents

When It Catches Up With You

It was a beautiful spring morning. As I slid into the front seat of my car, I noticed a cardinal singing in a tree in my back-yard. The cardinal may have been happy about the new day, but I wasn't. My breathing was labored and I was weary to the bone. I'd felt lousy for several weeks.

A reporter and copy editor at a daily newspaper, I had a busy work, family, and church schedule—too busy to pay attention to the warnings my overweight and overburdened body was trying to give me. Besides my demanding, six-days-a-week job at the newspaper, I did some free-lance magazine writing on the side. I was a member of my church's worship group and traveled to prisons throughout the state with a prison music ministry. All during this time my wife was complaining that she and I were becoming strangers. But I felt so bad that I spent most of my time running or coping with fatigue.

In the weeks following that spring day, I grew progressively fatigued. Some mornings I could barely get my feet out of bed. My job performance suffered because I couldn't concentrate. At the end of the day I found myself coming home and collapsing in an easy chair until I stumbled off to bed at nine or ten.

Still I tried to ignore my condition. After all, in college I'd often worked on the student newspaper forty hours a week while carrying a full class load and keeping busy with various nonacademic involvements. In high school, I'd jump from football weight-training sessions to marching-band practice without needing a moment's rest between.

But those days were long gone, I discovered.

By summer I began to have dizzy spells and sometimes struggled for breath. I went to several physicians but didn't get much relief. My condition continued to deteriorate. Then the roof fell in. In August I was diagnosed with asthma, severe allergies, out-of-control diabetes, dangerously high blood pressure, and a seriously compromised immune system. Every month I got weaker, until I was severely ill. For the first time in my life, I experienced psychological depression. Life became an ordeal rather than a blessing. I wondered how much courage and strength I had left. How long could I cope with the pain and mind-numbing fatigue I was living with each day?

My condition came to a head one day when I nearly collapsed after playing the trumpet during a Sunday morning church service. My wife and friends nearly had to carry me to my car. My life had "bottomed out" and my health was on the skids.

Obviously I'm still alive to tell you my story. With guidance from a natural health and nutrition counselor, I began a series of changes that have brought about many wonderful improvements in my life. These simple but critical changes involved adjustments in nutrition, physical activity, social interaction, and work habits.

Most important—and the reason I'm writing this book for you—I became painfully aware of the fragility of the human body. I realized that no man can take his health for granted. I gradually moved toward a more healthy way of living and developed an almost evangelical passion for helping others learn some simple secrets for a healthful lifestyle. I enrolled in school again and earned a degree in nutrition. Now I combine free-lance writing with an individual natural health and nutritional counseling ministry. My health has improved substantially and I've lost seventy-five pounds of excess baggage. My wife and I are enjoying some of the best years of our lives together. I can once again look to the future with hope rather than despair.

I'll tell you more about how I found my way through the maze of chronic illness to better physical, spiritual, and emotional health later in this book. But before I go into the specifics of how I worked my way out, I want to talk to you about *your* health. Perhaps you are one of the thousands of men who are feeling run-down and depleted, admitting to yourself and to others that you simply don't have the stamina you had ten years ago.

If you are tolerating or ignoring warning signs (as I once did) and taking your health for granted, you are putting yourself at greater risk than you can imagine. By ignoring a need for diet and exercise, many put themselves at risk of dying of a heart attack or stroke. Many fall victim to emotional turmoil and a general sense of hopelessness, seeking comfort in addictions such as drugs, alcohol, food, and sexual voyeurism.

Today's American male is suffering from chronic stress. We are conditioned by a culture—even our church culture—that teaches us that a man's value is best expressed in what he can produce or accomplish.

Many of us, too, have been taught that we are not allowed to admit to feelings of vulnerability, insecurity, depression, or anxiety. Despite the current wave of openness about emotions, most men still believe we have no right to feel anything—at least not to show it. As a result, we don't allow ourselves the "luxury" of allocating time to attend to physical, emotional, and spiritual maintenance issues. We carry internally the burden of providing for our families, taking care of our cars and homes, and being successful in our careers. As a result, we have little time left to focus on the important needs of body and soul.

Maybe you're not experiencing a crisis—but smaller problems are a chronic nuisance, such as stiff joints, constant indigestion, sleep disturbances, and mood swings. You don't have to wait to make healthy choices now that will create for you a better-quality life, and maybe a longer one. In fact, based on my own experiences, I highly recommend that you *don't* wait for a crisis before you begin to make changes.

In the pages to follow, I will explore the most important aspects of self care and do it from a man's perspective. Books have been written about specific subjects such as nutrition, exercise, and how to handle the stresses and strains of life. This book is written to give you a way to look at all of your potential as a human being. It will help you assess what you need most and set up a simple plan to help you make even a few important steps to improve your health and well-being.

Though most self-care books tend to be for women, this one is especially for men.

Do any of these men sound like you?

Stan

At age forty-one, Stan is at the height of his law career. To fully satisfy the needs of his demanding but high-paying clients, he often finds himself working fifteen-hour days.

Lately Stan has been forced to spend more time at the office on weekends, and he's been sneaking in an hour or so before church on Sunday mornings to get some things done. A cross-country runner in his high school and college days, now Stan's weight has steadily climbed to 230 pounds. Exercise is an occasional outdoor walk with his daughters. Lunch is often a cheeseburger and fries while on the run.

One evening Stan is sitting in front of the television set watching football, when he notices an aching sensation and pressure in his chest. His left arm hurts and he feels a little short of breath. *Must have been that pizza we had for supper*, he rationalizes. In a moment, it passes. Will Stan soon be visiting a hospital emergency room?

Tony

Tony is thirty-six. He has a good job as a pharmaceuticals salesman. But he has no time for himself and feels guilty if he takes any time away from his wife and two daughters. He seldom manages to sneak in a game of basketball or golf with his friends or even an evening out for dinner and a theater performance.

Awake at five A.M. most weekday mornings, Tony hits the road by six. A salesman must accept rejection as a part of the job, and Tony knows this, but sometimes it's still not easy to have a door slammed in your face. At church, Tony hopes to find acceptance and love. But this is hard to come by because "fellowship" on Sunday morning is a quick "hello," and the men's breakfasts are a lot of back-patting and talking about business.

Tony is often frustrated and disappointed that there seems to be no place where he can build friendships with other men who want to relax, talk honestly, and sometimes pull families together for a day of fun or shared Christian service. He wants something beyond sermons and bimonthly spaghetti suppers.

When the pressure pushes Tony to the breaking point, he stops at a neighborhood sports bar on the way home from work. Gradually, he's come to the point where he is relying on alcohol a lot. He doesn't dare bring this up with his Christian friends, though. What would they think?

Roger

An advertising company account executive with a fashionable home in the suburbs, Roger has a wife, two children, and a Basset hound. He's a member of the missionary board at his church and serves as an elder.

Roger's wife is the anxious type and pressures him to be at home unless he is working or involved in church functions. Roger, though a committed Christian for many years, has trouble smiling or laughing. He looks perpetually sad, as though he has just lost his best friend.

Chronic stomach problems and unexplained arthritic pains in his joints are just some of Roger's physical symptoms that something is amiss. He complains to other men that he feels trapped in his life but is afraid to communicate these feelings to his wife.

Roger's general outlook is growing progressively worse, and he sometimes wonders if he's seriously depressed. He has thoughts of "leaving it all" and running from his responsibilities. He has even had some thoughts of suicide. Roger feels like there is no way out. He sees no light at the end of the tunnel.

John

John is pastor of a large city church. He is almost universally esteemed as a preacher and teacher. John's church is growing and many have come to a personal relationship with Jesus Christ through John's ministry.

When John enters his church at the beginning of a workday, he is faced with an almost endless barrage of decisions to be made. His phone is constantly ringing with people who desperately need his help. Lately he has been feeling fatigued, and he went to the doctor last week to get some relief from his migraine headaches.

Sharon is young, attractive, and full of enthusiasm and energy. She is John's new secretary. While John's wife does little to build up her husband's self-esteem, the new secretary makes every effort to fortify John's faltering ego.

Daydreaming at his desk and glancing in the direction of his secretary's office, John realizes that Sharon makes him feel significant, accepted. And her youthful enthusiasm fires the sometimes waning sense of purpose in his life.

John tells himself that he can't help but fantasize about Sharon. But there is a growing chasm between his emotions—which tell him that this woman might be the answer to his growing discontentment—and his conscience, which tells him otherwise.

Tom

Tom is a man who is frustrated in his Christian walk. He feels drawn to help out drug addicts and hard-core drinkers at an inner-city ministry, but he just doesn't seem to be able to find the time—or the energy—to devote to Christian service. Tom wants his life to count for God and he's saddened when he thinks about how the years are speeding by. He knows he can't wait forever for his life to have more meaning and purpose but he doesn't know what to do about it.

Richard

Richard finds himself worrying about things he has never worried about before. At his last checkup, the doctor discovers Richard's blood pressure is somewhat above normal for his age and suggests that he monitor his pressure at home. Richard just can't seem to get his mind off the doctor's frank admonition: "Richard, hypertension can lead to heart disease and stroke if left untreated." *What is my life coming to?* he wonders.

Paul

Paul has been a successful insurance agent for many years. But at age forty-five he wonders if he is going through the stage of life characterized by pop psychologists as "male meno-pause." Paul is making a good living for his wife and three children but he doesn't seem to be finding much fulfillment in his work. Life is passing him by, he feels, and the good years are surely behind him. Paul would like to make some changes but he tells himself he is in no position to do so. "I don't want to uproot the family by making a big move," he tells his best friend. "That would be selfish of me, wouldn't it?"

All of these men have something in common. They are faced with the challenges of life that come with growing older. Some men are dealing with some of the more significant changes that often occur as we reach age forty-five and beyond.

If you're concerned about a minor or major aspect of your physical, emotional, and/or spiritual health and well-being, remember this: a simple tool can make a powerful difference. If you've ever used a dime instead of a screwdriver to attach a license plate to your car, you know what I mean. This book can be the "tool" you use to make powerful changes in many areas of your life.

Diet and Nutrition

Food and water are the fuels that feed our bodies as gasoline fuels our cars. Maybe you've settled into a pizza-and-burrito habit. It's a lot easier to grab a quarter-pounder at the fast-food restaurant than to take the time to fix a healthy meal. You may be wondering how those pizzas and burritos translate into the fact that at age thirty-five you have a "spare tire" for the first time in your life, and you're using the last hole on your favorite belt. In this book, you'll learn some simple tips on healthy eating that will help make it easier for you to make the right choices to provide the best fuel for your body.

Action

The weird guy with muscles in his toenails comes on your TV screen telling you that you can look *just like him* if you buy the Flab-Buster for $69.95 (which includes a free travel-hygiene kit). You've heard all of this many times before and it's made you become cynical about exercise programs. But you have been noticing that you don't seem to have the stamina you once had. You're ready for a breather after only a few minutes of full-court basketball with the guys after work. The doctor says your blood pressure is a little bit on the high side, and you'd like to be able to make it through the workweek with some energy to spare for the weekend.

In this book, I want to help you find the right exercise for you and your life-style. We may never see you on one of those cable television muscleman exhibitions, but you can improve your physical condition to the point where you have a new-found zest and enthusiasm for leading an active life.

A Network of Health-Giving Relationships

Women do seem to have a generally easier time communicating with each other on a level that transcends the superficial. But the man who has even one close friend with whom to blow off steam, relax, belly-laugh, catch a ball game, and vent worries about his work, marriage, and kids is doing himself a big favor. He is reducing the stress load in his life and giving himself an opportunity to have a better mental and emotional outlook.

Maybe you're so busy with your job and family that you haven't taken the time to really get to know other men. But sometimes you find yourself waking up in the middle of the night thinking, *Who could I depend on if I had a crisis in my life? Who would care enough to be willing to help me?*

Maybe you're carrying too much "emotional weight"—involving yourself with too many people who complain, criticize, and, well, really tend to drain you of energy and enthusiasm. And perhaps you're involved with too few people who build you up, encourage you, or share some of your interests.

Mark looks for support and encouragement from Christian brothers at church-related functions, but other men seem to be threatened at the prospect of being transparent and open with their own thoughts and feelings. Often Mark has considered sharing with other men his feelings of being alone and isolated, but he wonders if they'll think less of him. So he hides behind his mask and does the required glad-handing—offering various religious greetings that sound good but sometimes don't carry the weight of sincerity.

How does a man let down his guard and risk being honest enough to develop healthy relationships? How do you move beyond casual friendships into the realm of meaningful relationships with other men? Why are solid friendships with other Christian men important to your own emotional well-being and stability? We'll discuss these topics and other associated ones in the pages to come.

Begin Today!

Maybe you've never thought that taking care of yourself involved issues covering such a broad agenda. But matters of the heart and soul—as well as practical matters related to taking care of your body—are all important to living a well-balanced, happy life. An isolated and lonely person is often an unhappy and depressed person. This can open the door to serious emotional problems as well as physical problems. The two often go hand in hand.

In this book, we'll examine how you can develop lasting and meaningful friendships. We'll talk about confronting the past and how healing can take place in the present. We'll look at ways to reduce the stresses and strains in your life. And, of course, we'll explore in detail subjects such as nutrition and exercise, which are so important to your overall health and well-being.

Begin *now* to make positive changes in your life. Become committed to yourself because you're worth it! You're never too old, and it's never too late to start taking care of yourself. It's never too early to start replacing unhealthy habits with a new lifestyle that will keep you healthier and happier in the years to come. A famous baseball player probably reflected the sentiments of millions of men when he said, "If I'd known I was going to live this long, I would have taken better care of myself."

Today is the day to begin taking care of yourself. Choose to live your life to its fullest, leaving behind that health-robbing life-style and looking ahead to the many wonderful things God most certainly has in store for you!

For Thought and Discussion

1. Have you been taking care of yourself in recent months? If not, why not?
2. Have you been noticing any signs of your health being compromised? Do you have less energy than you once had? Are you sick more frequently? Do you find that you've lost some enthusiasm for living?
3. Can you see any of your own circumstances in the author's story before he had a serious health crisis?
4. What do you hope to gain from reading a book of this nature?

Over the Hurdles

Watch some of the weight-loss and exercise-product infomercials on television, and you will see talented actors and actresses who are virtual masters in the art of hype and oversell. They seem to be bubbling over with enthusiasm about the great results you're going to get from buying a product. But what they're *really* enthusiastic about is the money piling up in their personal bank accounts.

Becoming motivated and enthusiastic about making some changes in your life is certainly the first step in moving toward a more healthy way of living. But motivation alone isn't enough. You have to have goals and objectives, and you have to be determined to see them fulfilled in your life. Enthusiasm and hype aren't sufficient in and of themselves for the long haul. You need a plan and a purpose.

Many years ago a remarkable man lived in my community. Well into his seventies at the time, this man participated in long-distance runs throughout the United States. Often he'd stop in at the newspaper office where I worked to chat and, in a friendly manner, to badger me about my apathy when it came to anything having to do with physical fitness.

One of the sportswriters working on the newspaper staff at that time was probably in worse shape physically than I was. He lived on a steady diet of burritos, pizza, and beer and weighed upwards of 270 pounds. When it came to his physical health, this man was quite a skilled rationalizer. Let me elaborate.

One day the elderly distance runner dropped by our newspaper office and half-jokingly chided me about my steadily growing midsection. The sportswriter, who had never met a beef burrito he didn't like, began to parrot my friend, the distance runner.

"I really don't think you've got much room to talk, fella," I replied, smiling. His response brought the house down in the newsroom.

"Whaddya mean? I've been seriously thinking about getting on a good exercise program for over a year!"

Although I laughed along with the rest of the journalists, I could relate to the rationalizing sportswriter's expressed sentiment. Though many of us have the best of intentions about maintaining or improving our health and well-being, those intentions aren't always easy to put into practice.

Many obstacles stand in the way of a man's efforts to take care of himself. There are hurdles that exist between your ears. Let's take a look at some of them:

Perfectionistic Thinking

When it comes to matters of health and fitness, perfectionistic thinking can be a monumental obstacle. Many men stop short of beginning to make positive changes in their lives because they're looking for the perfect exercise, the best time, and a guarantee of complete and lasting success. In many ways, the diet and exercise perfectionist is simply afraid of failure, so he doesn't even try!

When I was a young man in my twenties, I was a stereotypical "yo-yo dieter." I'd develop a very rigid set of dietary standards and force myself to adhere to them religiously. After I'd lost forty or fifty pounds, I'd eventually develop a crack in my willpower and quit the rigid program. Then I'd gain back the weight I'd lost and a few extra pounds to boot.

I had much the same experience with fitness and exercise. I'd join a health club for a while or sign up for a local basketball league. For several weeks, sometimes several months, I'd exercise religiously. Then one night I'd feel tired and depleted and decide to forgo my visit to the health club. The next day guilt would set in, followed by a feeling of hopelessness. Because I'd fallen off the wagon for one night, I'd convince myself that it was pointless to try to continue with an exercise program. I'd "blown it," after all.

You may be thinking, *I'm worried that I won't be perfect in meeting my fitness goals* or *I won't stick with it.* So you don't even begin.

A biblical teaching provides us with a philosophical foundation for gaining control of our all-or-nothing thinking. Jesus told us to live life one day at a time.

"Therefore, do not worry about tomorrow, for tomorrow will worry about itself. Each day has enough trouble of its own" (Matthew 6:34).

I've found that the best way to overcome perfectionistic or all-or-nothing thinking is to focus on my goals in steps. I can control what I do *today*!

Here are some steps to get you started:

1. You can eat more vegetables, fruits, and grains and less fats and sugars.
2. You can exercise regularly, even if you start out by only walking around your neighborhood for half an hour two or three times a week.
3. You can take a good multivitamin and mineral supplement.

4. You can spend half an hour praying, reading the Word, and in quiet reflection.
5. You can readjust your priorities to set aside time to devote to taking care of yourself.

Should I happen to "blow it" on a given day when it comes to diet and exercise, I wake up the next morning to a new day and another chance to do what I know is best for me in the long run.

If you're a football fan like me, how many times have you seen this scenario take place during a game? Team A burns team B's defense on four straight pass plays and has a first and goal at team B's eight-yard line. But after three straight plays in which they gain virtually nothing, team A is forced to settle for a field goal.

If the defensive players on team B were all-or-nothing thinkers, they would have given up after team A got inside their ten-yard line. Instead, they deal with each play as it unfolds and manage to be successful in preventing a touchdown.

No matter how many times you "blow it," you can be successful in meeting your health and fitness goals—if you resolve to get back into the game. The big touchdown is not the point—health and a measure of fitness is.

My Life Runs Me

With all of the things I once had going on in my life, I often used the excuse that I didn't have the time to devote to taking care of myself because I had too many other things to do that were more important.

During the past few years, I've learned something about time demands. Some are necessary—especially those that involve one's job or upkeep on a home or an automobile. Other time demands are avoidable. To use an anti-drug campaign slogan of the '80s, we sometimes need to "Just Say No."

Most men have many responsibilities threatening to devour their time during any given week. They have a wife, children, job pressures, church-related duties, and often a big lawn to mow or a driveway to shovel. They may also have aging parents to help care for or to visit. Yes, these are big responsibilities and, yes, they do consume time and energy.

But have you ever done an inventory of your life to determine what you may be doing with that extra bit of time that you do have? Some of us have become overcommitted to our careers, to our churches, and even to our families. A few of us have been led to believe that we should be all things to all people all of the time!

What I've learned to do over the years is to establish my time priorities based upon my personal values. Maybe "John" will lose money and some of the good graces of his boss for turning down overtime work at the factory, but he'll be able to spend more time relaxing and having fun with his family.

I once heard a television pastor tell about some of his experiences in ministering to dying men in hospitals. "I've never once had one of these men tell me 'I wish I had spent more time at the office,' " said the pastor. "They always say something like, 'I wish I had spent more time with my family and friends'."

Take a look at what you are doing with your time. It is a valuable commodity and it passes by very quickly. Do a time inventory based upon what you perceive will have lasting value in your life. It helps to occasionally ask yourself some basic philosophical questions: "Why am I here? Why did God put me on this planet? What is my ultimate purpose in life and how can I better fulfill it?"

Why Devote Time to Self Care?

We men do have important God-ordained roles to play in our families as breadwinners, nurturers, leaders, and caretak-

ers. But as human beings we also have our own needs to consider. One of those needs is to devote the necessary time to
taking care of ourselves. For me, this must be a priority. And
it doesn't mean that we have to ignore our families while we're
doing it. Often I'll take my son along for my walks in the neighborhood and he enjoys the quality one-on-one time he gets
with his dad. I never communicate to my family the message
that the time I spend on health maintenance is more important
to me than they are. But they do get the message that I need
some time to take care of physical and emotional health issues.

Along with perceived time limitations, other barriers
standing in the path of a man deciding to begin to take care of
himself could best be characterized as attitudinal barriers.

Do you recognize any of the following unhealthy attitudes?

Ignore it and it will go away. This is nothing less than de-
nial, when a man notices that his health and peace of mind
are being compromised and he chooses to pretend that nothing is wrong. He hopes that he'll wake up some morning and
find his problems have simply gone away. To this kind of
thinking, let me say: Your problems will NOT go away. You're
going to have to do something!

Fatalist. This is the man who says that because his grandpa
died at fifty-eight he's doomed to a similar fate and there's no
use trying to avoid it. My word to this man: The central message of the Bible is that "all things are possible" to those who
have a relationship with God and faith in His plans for their
lives. Though hereditary factors do play a role in a man's
health, many of these hereditary vulnerabilities can be overcome with proper diet and exercise.

The religious rationalist. I can identify with this attitude
because I had it ten years ago. This guy may have one of several unbalanced attitudes. He may believe himself to be so
spiritual that he's lost interest in the temporal—"trivial"
things like taking care of his body. Why invest time maintain-

ing your physical health when the spirit is all that's going to last for eternity? He may also think that putting his family first means that he can never devote time to his own human needs.

I got rid of my religious rationalist attitude when I discovered that chronic ill health can put a Christian man on the sidelines because his body won't cooperate. Jesus, undoubtedly, was not a member of a health club, but the Bible portrays Him as a healthy, strong, and vigorous man.

Hey, I like my red meat and chocolate cake! I call this the stubborn attitude. This man doesn't want to make changes in his life-style because he likes things the way they are, and he doesn't want to give up any pleasures in his life. Listen up: I know a man just like you. He was in his forties when he had his first heart-bypass operation. Since then, he's decided that he'd much rather give up his double cheeseburgers than face another heart operation.

———

Now that we've discussed in detail some of the barriers that may stand in the way of a man realizing his self-care objectives, let's turn our attention to how we can successfully overcome some of those obstacles by setting realistic goals for ourselves.

Give Yourself a Chance to Succeed

First of all, you need to set out to give yourself the very best opportunity to be successful in reaching your objectives each and every day.

Many men shoot themselves in the proverbial foot when they set unrealistic goals for themselves. You may never again be in the shape you were in when you were eighteen and running high school cross-country. But you can improve your health and fitness to the point that you're able to enjoy life—and possibly extend the number of your days on this planet in the process.

When I had a health crisis several years ago, I weighed 275 pounds and must have had about 98.8 percent body fat. In trying to recover from my various illnesses and afflictions, I knew that I needed to begin to exercise regularly. But I also knew that I would be limited in the early stages of my exercise regimen by my weight and existing health problems. So I started out slowly with some very conservative goals. The first few weeks I set a goal of walking about a quarter of a mile three or four times a week. This was an attainable goal for me at the time and under those circumstances.

You, too, need to honestly look at your life's circumstances and existing limitations. Perhaps you don't have the time to devote to a two-hour workout daily at the local health club. But you could set a more reachable goal, such as walking a mile four days a week through your neighborhood. Maybe you don't want to adopt a vegetarian diet like I have, but you could make it your goal to eliminate red meat consumption by 50 percent and increase your intake of fresh fruits and vegetables.

As a middle-age man, my perspective about time-related issues has changed considerably. I used to look at life as a 100-yard dash that I had to sprint through. Now I approach my life as if I'm running a marathon. I've learned to set reasonable goals and then pace myself as I move toward them. Go ahead, call me a turtle! I don't mind. I just want to finish the race.

Avoid "Quick-Fix," Short-Term Solutions

In my view, realistic goal setting is also a matter of avoiding some quick-fix, pseudo solutions when it comes to health and fitness.

In recent years abdominal exercisers have been selling like

hotcakes. They support the upper part of the body when you're doing sit-ups. I have one of these exercisers and I've found it to be beneficial. But many people have had inflated expectations for this equipment because they've swallowed all of the promotional propaganda.

I recently read a newspaper account about a man who went to his doctor and told him that he was considering buying an abdominal exerciser. This fellow weighed in at about 300 pounds and had a major-league beer belly.

"The guy on TV said I could have 'killer abs' in two weeks if I get me one of those machines," the man told his physician. "Do you think it might take me three or four weeks?" The article didn't document the doctor's reply, but I think it may have been something like "Fat chance!"

Faddishness and quick-fix solutions to issues involving diet and nutrition can also be counterproductive. While a special diet of shrimp and egg whites might help you take some extra pounds off (if that's all you eat), will you continue to eat only shrimp and egg whites for the rest of your life? Taking weight off is the easy part. *Keeping* it off is the real challenge. You need to develop nutritional habits that you can live with for the long haul, not quick-fix solutions that can sometimes create more harm than good.

In the area of nutritional and herbal supplementation, I've been disheartened over the years to see so many Christians swallowing the idea that they can find a quick-fix solution in one particular product. On an almost weekly basis, I'm approached by someone who tells me that he is selling the one product that will work miracles in my life.

Forget a well-balanced and nutritious diet, they say. Forget exercise. Forget taking tried and true supplements such as a good multivitamin and mineral formula and extra vitamin C. Just take this heavenly elixir and all of your health problems will be solved. I hate to sound cynical, but I believe the sellers are more concerned about solving their financial problems than they are about solving your health problems. Beware of the miracle herbal formula or the miracle new substance that scientists have recently isolated and now comes to you for the amazingly low price of $59.95!

Yes, there is a possibility that some people have benefited from taking these products (probably often from the placebo effect). Many people who take these "miracle" supplements do end up losing a little weight—from the wallet region!

What areas of your life do you believe could stand some improvement? You may find it worthwhile to do a little inventory to help you target areas in which you hope to make some changes.

1. *Weight.* Maybe you've begun to get a spare tire around your middle at the age of thirty-five. Or perhaps you've already been losing the battle of the bulge for many years.

2. *Energy.* You don't seem to have the stamina you once had. You want to enjoy a more vital and vibrant life-style, but you find yourself constantly running out of gas.

3. *Relationships.* You can list several acquaintances, but few true friends on whom you can rely on for support and encouragement.

4. *Emotions (Mood).* Your wife has been complaining about your mood swings, and you often battle free-floating anxiety and depression. Sometimes you feel you are simply going through the motions of living.

5. *Spiritual.* When you embraced Jesus Christ as your Lord and Savior many years ago, you were excited about embarking upon your new life as a Christian. Now, in many ways, your spiritual life seems stagnant. You are lacking the passion and fire that once characterized your relationship with God.

You may be able to identify other areas of your life that you feel need some attention.

Turn Over a New Leaf Every Day

One final tip on setting and reaching your health and fitness goals: Avoid the "Second Week in January Syndrome." We all know men who neglect good health and nutrition practices throughout the year, but who annually decide to turn over a new leaf right after the holidays. These well-meaning folks go out and buy the latest expensive exercise equipment and the fanciest sweat suits at the sporting goods store. By mid-February they are hanging the expensive sweat suit on the handlebars of the new exercise machine and reentering themselves in the "Recliner Olympics."

Taking care of yourself is a thirty-days-a-month, twelve-months-a-year proposition. While it does require some self-discipline, it doesn't have to be a form of bondage in your life. Actually it can be quite enjoyable. Set some realistic goals for yourself and try to realize them one day at a time. If you falter, remember that tomorrow is another day. You'll have another opportunity to be successful when the next day's sun pops over the horizon.

For Thought and Discussion

1. What do you feel are the barriers keeping you from realizing your health and fitness goals? How can you overcome these barriers?

2. Are you a perfectionistic thinker with an all-or-nothing attitude about nutrition and fitness? Do you have any unhealthy attitudes that may be standing in your way?

3. What are some realistic and attainable goals that you could set for the next two or three months of your life in the areas of nutrition and fitness?

4. Make a list of your time demands for a week. Can you change some of your priorities in order to give yourself more time to devote to taking care of yourself?

Time Alone With God

Money can't do it. Your job can't do it. A Caribbean vacation can't do it. Even your family and friends can't do it. No, nothing this world has to offer can bring lasting peace, joy, and happiness into the heart and soul of a man.

We human beings were created to have a close and intimate relationship with our Father in heaven. Without this closeness and intimacy, we're like abandoned orphans on this planet. We need God's love and we need to experience it in a tangible way on a daily basis. Nothing in this world provides an acceptable substitute for spending time alone with God, allowing Him to communicate with us and to love us.

Though God has created us all with an inner need for times of intimacy with Him, how many Christian men actually take full advantage of the Father's beckoning to regularly come away with Him to a place where His Word and His guidance—even the awareness of His presence—can create stability and health for their souls?

Many men are so overwhelmed with earthly responsibilities that they tend to bring a rushed and harried mindset into their devotional times with God. In this way, spending time alone in God's presence becomes simply another obligation to meet at the beginning or end of a long and stress-filled day.

These men often crack open a Bible, read a couple of Scripture verses, and recite a brief and passionless prayer before they grab a cup of coffee and head out the door. Though they believe that they've fulfilled their spiritual obligation for the day, they haven't experienced any sense of having been loved, healed, restored, or revitalized by their heavenly Father.

God Wants to Meet With Us Daily

No matter when or where we decide that we need to meet with God, He is always faithful to come and spend time with us. The door is never closed and His answer is always yes when we ask Him to hear our prayers. If you're like me, you may sometimes have a too casual attitude about spending time alone with the Lord. After a couple of days of virtually ignoring Him, we'll start to notice some anxiety or depression creeping in and be reminded that life is entirely too difficult when it's handled alone.

But have you ever thought about the price Jesus Christ had to pay so that we can enter into the very presence of a Holy God? When I think about this, it troubles me that I sometimes take this privilege so casually.

The book of Hebrews tells us that Jesus' blood had to be shed to make a way for us to enter into the "Most Holy Place" of the living God.

> Therefore, brothers, since we have confidence to enter the Most Holy Place by the blood of Jesus, by a new

and living way opened for us through the curtain, that is, his body, and since we have a great priest over the house of God, let us draw near to God with a sincere heart in full assurance of faith, having our hearts sprinkled to cleanse us from a guilty conscience and having our bodies washed with pure water. (Hebrews 10:19–22)

Since the shedding of Jesus' blood opened the way for us to have full and complete intimacy with a holy God, we know that we have a right to enter into the very throne room of God—into His holy presence.

Too many men have been indoctrinated with what I call "religious methodism"—believing that a given formula (or method) will accomplish something in the spiritual realm. Grace reigns, not the law—men's rules, traditions, habits, and rituals. You can have a talk with your Maker anytime, anywhere.

God's Grace Brings Joy and Liberty

Religious legalism and a works-oriented mentality can distort our perception of who we are in Christ and give us an inaccurate picture of how God sees us.

Some Christian men I know are filled with guilt and shame. They ruminate and wring their hands about their perceived inadequacies and flaws and don't seem to be able to grasp the concept that they are forgiven and accepted by God. Though they have accepted Jesus Christ as Savior and Lord, they still believe that God is continually "sizing them up" and finding them worthy of condemnation and punishment.

Some Christian men I know are constantly trying to please God with a spiritual performance mentality. They burn themselves out by trying to do good works for God and by holding themselves to standards of conduct and behavior that are impossible for any human being to attain.

Other Christian men I know seem to be convinced that God is happy when they're miserable. These folks appear to believe that the abundant life Jesus told us about translates into a daily exercise in futility, frustration, and despair. Being perpetually troubled and beaten down, they believe, is the condition of any self-respecting Christian who aspires to true holiness and purity.

Those who believe that a relationship with God is a lifelong sentence to gloom, hardship, and bondage, would do well to consider the writings of St. Augustine, an African bishop who lived more than fifteen hundred years ago. In his *Confessions*, St. Augustine wrote that to know God is to experience a life filled with true joy.

"For there is a joy that is not given to the ungodly," he wrote, "but only to those who love you for your own sake, and you yourself are their joy. And this is the happy life—to rejoice in you and to you and because of you. This is the happy life; there is no other."[1]

Entering Into His Presence

Psalm 100, verse 4, can serve as a compass to show us the way into the presence of God, which is a place of joy and peace. We come into His presence with a thankful heart and a desire to praise Him for His goodness and mercy—for all the good things He's already done and for all the good things He's going to do in the future.

When we begin our time alone with God based upon the pattern of Psalm 100, it helps us to keep our focus on God as our loving Father in heaven, and it enables us to avoid the common habit of merely reciting a Christian "wants" list.

When I was a younger man and a young Christian, I used

to believe that spending time in God's presence meant doing a lot of talking to God and very little listening. I'd have my Bible and my prayer list, and I'd dutifully mark off each name on the list as I prayed. After I'd reached the end of the list and alerted God to all of my needs, I'd thank Him for listening to me and go back to my daily activities.

But later in life I began to come to an understanding that meeting with God involves an attitude of being willing to *listen* as much as it involves talking to God. It also involves being quiet enough to hear His voice and discerning enough to recognize that it is indeed His voice when He's trying to speak to me.

Any relationship involves two-way communication. Can you imagine having a relationship with another man in which you did all of the talking and he did all of the listening? When we listen to God, we're listening to the One who created the universe! It stands to reason that He might have something significant to say to us.

The Scriptures indicate that being quiet and waiting upon God enables us to receive a greater revelation of God's true nature. "Be still, and *know* that I am God," says Psalm 46:10 (emphasis mine). When you've learned to be still and listen to the voice of God speaking to your spirit, it's certainly not difficult to know when it's God's voice that you're really hearing.

As a young Christian man, I had a difficult time with the concept of God as a loving Father in heaven. My dad's generation of men had trouble demonstrating love and affection to their sons both physically and verbally. Based upon my conversations with younger men, I don't think this has changed much for the sons of the baby boomer generation.

Though I know now that my dad loved me, he never told me that he did. So I was left guessing most of my childhood. Like many men in his generation of World War II combat veterans, he was very stern and often very critical. I was never given the impression that my dad loved me unconditionally. So when I became a Christian, I had a difficult time understanding and receiving my eternal Father's love. I was ready to go out to the mission field—*any* mission field—to prove to God that I was willing to suffer so that I would be worthy of His love for me.

But as I got older, God began to reveal himself to me as One who is unlike any earthly father. As the years have gone by, I've become more able to see Him as a Father who loves unconditionally and who loves without measure.

Coming to know God as my Father literally changed my life. It has made me a better Christian, helping me to be more able to love other people without fear. My preschooler son knows what it is to have his dad hug and kiss him because it happens on a daily basis.

When I set aside time to spend alone with my heavenly Father, I know I'm going to be meeting with my Dad, who loves me and accepts me as his son. "For you did not receive a spirit that makes you a slave again to fear," says Romans 8:15–16, "but you received the Spirit of *son*ship. And by him we cry, '*Abba*, Father.' The Spirit himself testifies with our spirit that we are God's children" (first emphasis mine).

Every son needs his dad's undivided attention, and I know that I get myself into deep trouble if I don't climb up on the lap of my heavenly Father on a regular basis.

A man once told me that he believed that God "throws us into deep water and lets us sink or swim on our own." This, he explained, was his earthly father's pathetic approach to child-rearing. Thankfully this man has since come to know God as his Father, and he now recognizes his heavenly "Lifeguard" when he sees Him!

Bring a Pitcher, Not a Glass

When's the last time you had a good drink? Not a twelve-ounce can of pop, but a sixty-four-ounce belly buster? Jesus told the woman at the well (John 4:10–15) that there is water to drink that, up to that point in her life, she hadn't tasted. It is "living water," and it sustains all life in the spirit. To know God, to love Him, and to spend time in His holy presence is to drink of that living water.

"Everyone who drinks this water will be thirsty again," Jesus said to the perplexed yet thirsty woman, "but whoever drinks the water I give him will never thirst. Indeed, the water I give him will become in him a spring of water welling up to eternal life."

If you've ever seen a tired, thirsty horse approach a watering trough, you know that the animal doesn't take a few quick swigs of water and then move on. "Mr. Ed" takes his time. He drinks in long, lusty swallows, filling himself up until he is satisfied. A thirsty dog, on the other hand, is usually in a big hurry to slake his thirst. He'll run to a water bowl and lap up the water as quickly as he can, spilling it out all over the floor in the process.

When it comes to drinking the water Jesus referred to in His conversation with the woman at the well, I tend to want to try to follow the horse's example. To be satisfied, I need to give myself plenty of time to spend in God's presence.

When we drink of the living water, we actually get a taste of eternal life in this parched and dying world, our temporary home. Why would anyone want to be in a hurry?

Transforming Power

Spending time alone daily in the presence of God can literally change a man's life. Consider Moses. When he came down from Mount Sinai with the two tablets of the Testimony in his hands, the Bible says that his "face was radiant [shining] because he had spoken with the Lord" (Exodus 34:29).

Your face may not literally shine after you've been in the presence of the Lord, but your life will. Spending time alone with God gives us a greater assurance of His never-ending and unfailing love. It changes our priorities, helps us to keep our focus on things of eternal consequence, and refreshes and re-vitalizes us physically, emotionally, and spiritually.

When is the last time you spent some time alone with your Father? He's been waiting for you.

For Thought and Discussion

1. Is having "quiet time" alone with God each day a priority for you? Are you willing to set aside time daily to spend with God?
2. Is your agenda flexible when you get alone with God? Will you relinquish control to Him?
3. Do you have any difficulty receiving the Father's love based upon your particular childhood experiences?
4. Thinking back on past occasions when you've spent time alone with God, how have these meetings with your Creator changed your life?

Notes

1. Rex Warner translation, *The Confessions of St. Augustine* (New York: Mentor Books, 1963), 232.

The "Food Fight"

For the first thirty-five years of my life, I never met a bacon cheeseburger I didn't like. That was my nutritional philosophy in a nutshell.

My diet was pretty much consistent with what has been coined the SAD diet—the Standard American Diet. The SAD diet is top-heavy with animal fats, sugars, packaged and frozen foods, and dairy products. It includes minimal amounts of fruits, vegetables, and complex carbohydrates.

The Standard American Diet has made us a nation of overweight men with high cholesterol and clogged arteries. The Standard American Diet is killing many of us!

When I was a boy, we frequently visited my grandparents in a rural area in southern Indiana, about forty miles from my home. My grandmother's meal preparation traditions were, not surprisingly, from the "old school," as were those of most grandmothers in the 1960s.

She would often fix batter-dipped fried chicken, mashed potatoes and gravy, homemade biscuits with real butter and preserves, candied sweet potatoes, baked beans, cottage cheese, and corn. After everyone had eaten themselves to the point of stupor, she would clear the table. Then she brought out the desserts: home-baked pies, custards, chocolate cake, homemade doughnuts, and ice cream.

Like everyone else, I ate all my stomach could hold. Then, after a brief respite, I'd raid Grandmother's pantry and have seconds and thirds of every dessert. This made her smile.

As you might expect, my grandparents were overweight. All of the members of my immediate family have struggled with weight problems. Though my mother, a registered nurse, tried to warn us about the consequences of bad eating habits, we paid little attention to her.

Moderately overweight as an adolescent, I became obese in college where the cafeteria fare of the 1970s was high fat, highly refined carbohydrates, and plenty of sugars. After college, my weight began to bounce around like a basketball. I'd balloon up to nearly three hundred pounds, then go on a crash starvation diet and lose seventy or eighty pounds. I did manage to lose over one hundred pounds while I was in my mid-twenties and, by eating two minuscule meals a day, kept most of it off for five years.

When I fell off the proverbial wagon soon after I was married, I quickly gained back all the weight I'd kept off for five years. Through my late twenties and early thirties, most of my meals came from a drive-thru window. I ate for taste—and it kept me obese and fatigued. My cholesterol levels were in the "danger" category by the time I was in my late twenties.

Now my diet consists mostly of fresh vegetables, fruits, grains, complex carbohydrates, and legumes, and I've replaced much of the fat in my body with muscle. I'm no longer eating for taste only, and I'm not in a state of nutritional ignorance and apathy.

The Error of Dietary Legalism

Before I go on, let me warn you of the error of what I call "dietary legalism." The dietary legalist is a person who says he never deviates from healthy nutritional habits, not even to eat a piece of cake at a relative's birthday party or a piece of pizza while supervising a youth group's all-nighter. There is nothing wrong with having an occasional fast-food burger, a couple of pieces of pizza, or a wedge of pie. This will not hurt you, and is even a better way to maintain good nutrition habits in the long run.

My weight-loss and weight-management efforts fifteen years ago didn't work because I tried to make them work on the basis of dietary legalism. It is better, healthier, and more effective to look at weight management as a way of living for the long haul. Diets don't work when you approach them with a legalistic, pass/fail, black-and-white, all-or-nothing mind-set. You don't want to become discouraged with the rigid constraints of a diet and then backslide into eating too many of the wrong things.

Always remember: You can promote both emotional and physical health by allowing yourself the "indiscretion" of infrequently allowing yourself a "forbidden" food.

Good Nutrition Is a Matter of Common Sense

Every dietitian or nutritionist has his or her own theory about health-promoting eating habits. I've read literally hundreds of them. Some of their theories are, I believe, far too permissive. They allow for too much animal product consumption and too many refined simple carbohydrates and sugars. On the other extreme are the nutritionists who want us to eat nothing but organic vegetables, brown rice, and tofu. Though the second approach would make more sense to me than the first, how many people—other than health food store proprietors—would be willing to make such drastic dietary sacrifices?

Good nutrition can be moderate and based on good re-

search, common sense, and biblical truth. It is important to
point out that those who have ongoing health problems
should always consult with their nutritionally aware physician before making major changes in their diets. Sometimes
one size doesn't fit all when it comes to nutritional needs.

Some Christian nutritionists suggest that God provided
certain foods for nutrition and for sustaining health and didn't
intend for us to eat certain other foods. Consider the following
passage in Genesis:

> Then God said, "I give you every seed-bearing plant
> on the face of the whole earth and every tree that has
> fruit with seed in it. They will be yours for food. And
> to all the beasts of the earth and all the birds of the air
> and all the creatures that move on the ground—every-
> thing that has the breath of life in it—I give every green
> plant for food." And it was so. (Genesis 1:29–30)

In later biblical accounts, God allowed man to kill and eat
animals. But God's original plan for sustaining life did not include eating animals and animal products. I believe this is because God knew eating animals would not be the healthiest
practice for humankind.

Animal Fat Causes Heart Disease and Other Illnesses

Animal products contain cholesterol and fat, which clog
the arteries and cause heart attacks. There is also some research that would indicate that animal fat can play a role in
the development of some cancers.

"Meat has several strikes against it," observes Harvard
Medical School-educated physician and author Andrew Weil,
M.D. In his book *Spontaneous Healing*, Weil says that meat "is
a major source of saturated fat in the diet, as well as a highly

concentrated form of protein. Being high on the food chain, it accumulates environmental toxins. Unless it is raised organically, it is also full of added toxins."[1]

Many farmers feed livestock a variety of antibiotics, chemicals, and hormones. These substances can concentrate in the flesh of the animal, which we consume. I don't know about you, but that's a discomforting thought for me.

You may not be inclined to want to change to a vegetarian diet. But you can easily reduce your intake of animal products. Begin by eating only very limited amounts of red meat products and pork and more of poultry and fish sources of protein. If you're more aggressive about change, focus your diet around fish. It's important that you adopt changes you can live with for the long haul.

Sugar Is Sweet, But Not Good for You

Another food substance that many nutrition experts believe should be consumed in very limited amounts is sugar. According to James F. Balch, M.D., and Phyllis A. Balch, C.N.C., sugar intake is thought to be a factor in many diseases.[2]

The Balches believe that a meal high in both sugars and animal fats will make you feel tired and lessen your ability to think properly because body tissues are not receiving enough oxygen. "Cravings for sweets can and should be satisfied with fresh fruit," they instruct. "Many fruits are sweet to the taste and are easy to digest. They also contain valuable nutrients that are necessary for good health."

Avoiding Food Additives

Living in our modern society, it is difficult to avoid the additives, preservatives, and taste enhancers many companies pump into their food products.

These preservatives and taste enhancers are man-made chemicals that you are introducing into your body. Most of these chemicals were invented in the modern era. Our great grandparents ate foods that were unadulterated by chemical preservatives and taste enhancers. It's a shocking statistic to consider that approximately 70,000 new chemicals have been introduced into our society since World War II—many of which have been added to our foods.[3]

If I had the time and the money, I'd buy all of my food fresh from the organic farmer's fields (where no pesticides are used)—so that I wouldn't be consuming foods that have been treated with preservatives and taste enhancers. Maybe your circumstances are as limited as mine—but we can shop and eat healthier with some easy adjustments.

Shop the Perimeter

I gravitate toward the outer aisles of the supermarket, where I can find the fresh fruits and vegetables. Yes, many of these food products have been treated with pesticides, but I use a pesticide-removing spray product to clean these foods before my family eats them. One prominent home shopping network sells this product and it can also be found in many health food stores and in some supermarkets.

Salt

It is unwise to consume much table salt. Too much salt in the system can cause fluid build-up in body tissues that can contribute to high blood pressure. The increase of water in the tissues can also make the essential process of waste excretion more difficult for the body to manage.[4]

As a rule, it is not a good idea to add salt to foods while cooking, either. You'll get plenty of salt in packaged and processed foods that you eat. If your doctor tells you that your high blood pressure may be connected to eating too much salt, read food product labels closely. Almost all foods purchased at fast-food restaurants are high in salt content.

If you want a salt substitute, consider kelp. This is a type of seaweed that has been used in the treatment of thyroid problems because it contains iodine. It can be purchased in granulated form, powder form, or as a tablet.

Pure Water

On planning for a trip to an underdeveloped country, perhaps you've received the warning, "Don't drink the water." But you don't have to travel to an impoverished country to find water that's not safe enough to drink. Just turn on the tap in your home! Water from household faucets is often from ponds, creeks, streams, rivers, and lakes. A variety of chemicals find their way into these water bodies and possibly into the water coming out of your faucet.

In order to purify drinking water, many municipalities add a number of potentially cancer-causing chemicals into the water supply.[5] There is also concern about the various kinds of bacteria and viruses that find their way into the public (and private—through water wells) drinking supplies.

There are a variety of systems and devices available on the market that will help you reduce pollutants in your drinking supply. See the sidebar.

There are three popular types of home water purification systems. You've probably seen many of the systems that use carbon filters in your local supermarket. These are often sold as water pitchers or carafes. Carbon filtration, the least expensive alternative in most cases, eliminates many—but not all—contaminants. Reverse osmosis devices are generally thought to be preferable to carbon filtration, but plastics used in some of those systems might leach into the water that is being purified.

Of the three systems, many health professionals believe that steam-distilling systems are the best alternative. In steam distillation, the steam rises and leaves behind most bacteria, viruses, and chemical pollutants. The steam then moves into a condensing chamber where it is cooled and condensed to become distilled water.

Steam-distilling systems do have some drawbacks. In the first place, they're expensive. The boiling chamber has to be cleaned frequently and it takes some time to purify relatively small amounts of water. But for your family's health and well-being, you may decide that a distilling system is worth both the expense and the trouble.

If you believe that the water in your home is safe and you don't have any qualms about drinking it, then you should take at least one precautionary step. Contact your local health department and ask how you can have your tap water tested for possible contamination. In many communities, there are laboratories that will test water to determine if it has been contaminated.

A Healthy Nutritional Foundation

What you and I need to do is to build our eating habits on a strong and healthy foundation—basing our consumption of foods on those that contribute most to health, physical strength, mental clarity, and emotional stability.

Meet Most of Your Protein Needs Through Plant Foods

As I mentioned before, there are many health drawbacks to a meat-based diet. S. I. McMillen, M.D., a Christian physician, points out that countries such as the United States—whose population mainly meets its protein needs with meat consumption—have a high rate of death from coronary artery disease. In countries where very little animal fat is consumed, atherosclerosis is rare.[6]

I decided to try a vegetarian diet after blood tests revealed that I had high cholesterol. I had already reduced my meat consumption to only fish and poultry, but apparently that wasn't enough to reduce my blood fats. So about two years ago I went to a total vegetarian diet.

There are times when a bacon cheeseburger still looks tempting. But for the most part I really don't miss eating meat. There are many meat substitutes, many vegetable proteins and grains that are almost as tasty as the real thing. Some of the substitutes, by the way, can be found in the frozen food sections of most grocery stores.

If you do eat meat, I urge you to try to avoid meat products that contain sodium nitrite or sodium nitrate. These food additives, which many health experts believe may cause cancer, are found primarily in bacon, ham, hot dogs, lunch meats, and cooked fish.

Should you someday decide in favor of a vegetarian diet, you may want to first consult with a nutritionally aware physician—particularly if you have any ongoing health problems. Also, most vegetarians take a good multivitamin and mineral supplement to compensate for some of the nutrients they won't be obtaining from meat.

At this point some of you may be saying to yourself, *This guy is nuts. I'm not going to give up my Thanksgiving turkey!* Though I believe that a vegetarian diet is the best diet for me, I realize that the majority of men are going to have little interest in such a radical departure from conventional eating habits. However, I would urge you to consider making your diet less dominated by meat products.

Try experimenting with some "meatless meals" on occasion. Buy a vegetarian pizza covered with tasty vegetables and lowfat cheese rather than one swimming in animal fat. Instead of getting a cheeseburger at a restaurant, try ordering the special turkey burger sandwiches offered by some. If you like meat for breakfast, eat grilled chicken breast instead of bacon, along with your multi-grain bread and cooked cereal.

Whatever kind of diet you choose, make sure it is high in fiber and complex carbohydrates, and low in fat and sugars. You can consume liberal amounts of foods such as fresh vegetables and fruits, salads, whole grains, rice, beans, baked potatoes, multi-grain cereals, and tofu.

"The people in cultures today who eat foods high in complex carbohydrates are essentially free of heart disease and strokes," says Christian physician Reginald Cherry, M.D., in his book *The Doctor and the Word.*[7] "Often their diets contain as much as 80 percent carbohydrates."

Dr. Cherry suggests the following high-carbohydrate nutritional groups should make up the substance of one's dietary intake, providing your body with the vitamins and minerals and dietary roughage it needs to function properly. These include green and yellow vegetables, grains, fruits, beans and peas. People often ask me to specify what foods they should eat in these food categories. I'll list some of them for you:

Fruits
These include apples (two or three a day), apricots, bananas, berries, cherries, dates, figs, grapefruit, grapes, melons, nectarines, oranges, peaches, pears, pineapples, plums, tangelos, and tangerines.

Vegetables
These include artichokes, asparagus, beets, broccoli, mushrooms, onions, parsnips, Brussels sprouts, cabbage, carrots, cauliflower, peas, potatoes, radishes, spinach, celery, corn, eggplant, garlic, bean sprouts, alfalfa sprouts, squash,

green beans, kale, leeks, lettuce, lima beans, turnips, yams, avocado, cucumber, peppers, and uncooked tomatoes.

Grains

These include multi-grain breads, rolls, and biscuits; rye bread, whole wheat bread, brown rice, bran and grain cereals, basmati rice, wild rice, whole grain crackers, rice cakes, honey sweetened or unsweetened granola, honey graham crackers, buckwheat pancakes and waffles (any other non-white flour pancake and waffle mix), artichoke pasta, corn pasta, sesame pasta, vegetable pasta, and whole wheat pasta.

Beans and Peas (Legumes)

These include tofu (used as a substitute for meat), black-eyed peas, garbanzo beans, great northern beans, kidney beans, lentils, mung beans, navy beans, pinto beans, and split peas.

In general, it is a good idea to consume dairy products in only very limited amounts due to their fat content, and because many milk cows are fed antibiotics and growth hormones that some experts believe may contaminate milk products. Any dairy products consumed should be lowfat versions such as skim milk, one percent cottage cheese, and lowfat and low-cholesterol cheese products.

Sweeteners should be used in limited amounts. These include honey, date sugar, and maple sugar. Avoid all artificial sweeteners as much as possible. Avoid carbonated drinks as much as possible, and consider replacing them with homemade carbonated drinks: mix fruit juice with Perrier or other bottled water.

Stocking the Fridge and Pantry

Back in your college days, you'd open your dorm room refrigerator to find "nutritious" foodstuffs like cold pizza from the night before, a few cans of soda pop, a jar of pickles, bologna, and a bottle of ketchup.

Now you're older and probably wiser. Here are some healthful foods to keep stocked in your refrigerator, freezer, and pantry.

You'll want to make certain your refrigerator always has a plentiful supply of fresh fruits and vegetables. Eating fresh, uncooked vegetables will provide your body with many more nutrients than you would get from cooked or canned vegetables. When you do cook vegetables, use a steamer to retain as many nutrients as possible.

Don't overdo it on milk products. Buy lowfat versions of margarine and cheese, and skim milk. If you're concerned about cholesterol in eggs, use an egg-substitute product.

If you eat meat, choose chicken, turkey, and fish whenever possible. Organically grown meats are even better because the animals aren't fed hormones, antibiotics, and other chemicals.

Olives and pickles are good treats (in moderate amounts because of the high sodium content) along with fruit juices (no added sugar). Keep lowfat cheese in the fridge for snacking, along with radishes, baby carrots, broccoli, and cauliflower.

Keep frozen yogurt, frozen fruit bars, frozen whole-grain waffles, and bagels in the freezer. You can even make some healthy meals ahead and keep in the freezer for when you and your wife are too busy to cook. Commercially made veggie burgers, "sausages," and "chicken" patties are great to have on hand. They cook up quickly, are quite tasty, and are lower in fat and cholesterol than the real thing.

Whole-grain cereals and crackers, buckwheat pancake mix, whole-grain breads, brown rice, and baking potatoes are good foods to stock in your pantry. Keep canned tuna, lowfat soups, natural or reduced-fat peanut butter, jellies and jams made with fruit and fruit juice only, lowfat popcorn, fruit leathers, and lowfat cheese products on hand, as well. Besides your fresh and frozen fruits and vegetables, you may want to keep a few cans of fruit in its own juice and vegetables for backup when your fresh supply is down.

Keep Twinkies and Ho-Hos in the grocery store where they belong!

What About Eating Out?

One of the biggest frustrations for me, as I try to eat as healthy as possible, is going to a restaurant—particularly a fast-food restaurant. It's difficult to get a meal that isn't inundated with food preservatives, slathered in animal fat, or laden with sugar to the point of being sickeningly sweet.

Here are four suggestions that can help make eating out more healthy for you:

1. *Eat out less often.* Many of us can fall into a habit of eating out too often, which is expensive and not as health promoting as taking the time to prepare nutritious meals at home. Make eating out a special occasion.

2. *Gravitate toward the salad bar.* Usually you can find plenty of fresh fruits and vegetables and even bean salads in the salad bar.

3. *Look for healthy main dishes.* These could include chicken and fish that are not fried, vegetarian pizza, pasta dishes, baked potatoes stuffed with vegetables and lowfat sour cream or yogurt, fruit salads, and whole-grain breads.

4. *Eat less.* Whether I'm eating at a restaurant or at home, I've found that I feel better when I consume small but frequent meals. This puts less stress and strain on the body. It doesn't have to work as hard to digest and metabolize food when it comes in smaller quantities.

As I mentioned before, though, it is often counterproductive to engage in "dietary legalism." Treats should be allowed occasionally, and there are even times—such as Thanksgiving Day or a family birthday—when it's okay to eat more than your usual fare. Simply resume your healthy diet the next day.

Other Health-Promoting Foods

Olives and Olive Oil

These foods are mentioned frequently in the Bible. Recent research indicates that olive oil can lower blood cholesterol and blood pressure. Olive oil is rich in vitamin E, a powerful antioxidant. It can be used as a substitute for other oils that are high in saturated fat. You may already know about high-fat tropical oils (palm and coconut), butter, and lard. But Dr. Weil also warns against the use of polyunsaturated vegetable oils such as corn and safflower. He recommends eliminating them from the diet[8] and using olive oil, the "best and safest of all edible fats."

Yogurt

Many Bible scholars believe that what was called sour or curdled milk (curds) in antiquity may have been similar to what we now call yogurt. Though some milk products consumed in large quantities may pose a threat to good health, yogurt has many health-sustaining properties. The acidophilus in yogurt helps to maintain a balance between the "good" and "bad" bacteria that are present in our bodies—particularly in our digestive system. That's why many physicians recommend yogurt to a patient who is taking antibiotics (which kill off good bacteria as well as the targeted bad bacteria).

Recent studies have pointed to many yogurt benefits, including its capacity to boost the immune system, improve bowel function, help prevent heart disease, and help prevent colon and other types of cancer.

Fish

Fresh fish was a staple of life in New Testament times and undoubtedly a food savored by Jesus during His time on earth.

Omega–3 fatty acids found in fish make it a particularly health-sustaining food. Fish is a rich source of protein and also provides many essential vitamins and minerals. Studies indicate that eating fish can help lower cholesterol, reduce blood triglycerides, lower blood pressure, reduce risk of heart disease, inhibit cancer, help regulate the immune system, and help ease symptoms of arthritis.

Fish that are harvested from cold, deep water are thought to be the best source for omega–3 fatty acids. These include salmon, mackerel, herring, sardines, lake trout, whitefish, bluefin tuna, and anchovies. (By the way, if you can't stomach fish, Dr. Weil recommends flax seeds, flax meal, and flax oil for omega–3 needs.)

There are many other foods that have been recognized since Bible times as being health sustaining—such as barley, garlic, onions, lentils, wheat, honey, figs, lamb, cucumbers, grapes, nuts, and melons.

God has provided us with enough good foods to eat that no one need be deprived of sensory pleasure to be healthy, and neither does anyone need to be constantly hungry to be healthy. It is more a matter of acquiring a taste for the foods that are good for you. Eat on! But eat good, *nutritious* food.

For Thought and Discussion

1. Would you be willing to change some dietary habits if you knew doing so would add to the quality of your life and possibly extend your time on this earth? How far are you willing to go?
2. Have you ever noticed a connection between what you eat and how you feel?
3. Were you raised in a family that paid little attention to proper nutrition? Do you remember ever having a discussion about nutrition with your parents or other family members when you were a child?
4. What Scriptures in the Bible can you find that address issues relating to nutrition? Do you think God might have intended that we learn some truths about nutrition from His Word?

Notes

1. Dr. Andrew Weil, M.D., *Spontaneous Healing* (New York: Alfred A. Knopf, Inc., 1995), 147.
2. Dr. James F. and Phyllis A. Balch, *Prescription for Nutritional Healing* (Garden City Park, N.Y.: Avery Publishing Group, Inc., 1990), 14–15.
3. Nancy Sokol Green, *Poisoning Our Children* (Chicago: The Noble Press, Inc., 1991), 13.
4. *Prescription for Nutritional Healing*, 14.
5. Ibid., 25.
6. S. I. McMillen, M.D., *None of These Diseases* (Old Tappan, N.J.: Fleming H. Revell Co., 1984), 144.
7. Reginald Cherry, M.D., *The Doctor and the Word* (Orlando, Fl.: Creation House, 1996), 77–78.
8. Dr. Weil, *Spontaneous Healing*, 140–142.

Exercise
(Move It or Lose It)

Every health maintenance plan needs to include exercise. You can diet and lose 100 pounds in six months. But if regular exercise is not a part of your weight-loss regimen, your overall health is not likely to improve. God created our bodies to be *used* on a daily basis. Muscles that aren't used at all atrophy. We were made to be in motion.

Heart of the Matter

Fitness experts tell us that every man can benefit from getting some regular aerobic exercise—that is, sustained exercise that increases the body's ability to deliver oxygenated blood to muscles and organs. Some of these exercises include brisk walking, jumping rope, cross-country skiing, cycling, rowing, jogging, and swimming. The most aerobically valuable activities are those that produce a high heart rate and a demand for large amounts of oxygen that can be sustained for long periods.[1]

Fitness experts differ on how much aerobic exercise we

need. The middle-ground viewpoint seems to be that we should aim for at least thirty minutes of aerobic exercise four to five times a week.

Dr. Charles Serritella, a chapter contributor to the book *The Best of Total Health*, explains the benefits of regular aerobic exercise as follows:

> A regular three-mile daily walk enhances the efficiency of our cardiovascular and respiratory systems. Heart and blood vessels are helped and blood pressure tends to become normalized. The lungs and entire respiratory tract are improved as well as the organs, tissues, and tissue cells. The brain can function better because of the accelerated removal of wastes from the blood and the influx of oxygen and needed nutrients into the millions of individual brain tissue cells.
>
> After a refreshing walk and a shower, we are exhilarated for our daily tasks, and we're not nearly as pooped at the end of the day. Believe it or not, even our relations with others improve because we feel better. Here is a "high" without drugs or alcohol.[2]

You probably don't need much more convincing about the value of regular exercise. But you may be unsure about how to begin an exercise program. Let's talk about some of the elements involved.

Attitude

When I began to exercise on a regular basis, I had to change my attitude about exercise. Instead of viewing it as some sort of self-induced punishment, I had to begin to see exercise as something that I *wanted* to do to improve my health.

You, too, might need an "attitude check." Perhaps you're a guy who comes home from work dog tired. Your wife reminds you that the doctor told you to get some regular exercise. Your response: "I work too hard and I don't have time for it." Maybe you're a man who has a sedentary job, sitting at a desk all day. You erroneously believe that another relatively sedentary activity—such as fishing or spectator sports—will meet your exercise needs.

The first guy is tired because he isn't getting enough aerobic exercise. Regular aerobic exercise *increases* energy levels. He could also find half an hour for some aerobic activity every day—even if it meant missing the first quarter of a football game on the tube—if he is really motivated to do so. The second guy is only kidding himself if he thinks sedentary activities can replace regular aerobic exercise.

I didn't begin an exercise program because someone else told me I should or because of guilt. I did it because I wanted to be good to myself. Exercise time should be something that we look forward to, not something we dread. Develop realistic expectations and goals. Be patient with yourself as you gradually see your levels of fitness improve over time.

Commitment

Once you've made a decision to begin an exercise regimen, you may want to inventory your commitment to the program. Do want an easy regimen, a moderate regimen, or do you want to go all the way for a heavy-duty commitment that could involve intensive muscle-building sessions and grueling aerobic workouts at a local gym?

Many fitness experts say that it is better to make a small commitment (especially to start with) and follow through on it than to make a bigger commitment and not fulfill it. Let's take a look at three of these exercise commitment levels:

Low exercise. This could involve something as simple as taking a brisk walk every day for an hour, a few stretching exercises, sit-ups, and other mild forms of working your muscles.

Moderate exercise. This could involve a brisk daily walk, stretching exercises and sit-ups, along with tennis and/or racquetball sessions once or twice a week.

High exercise. This could involve aggressive aerobic work-outs—such as distance-running and cycling—and muscle-building weight-lifting programs in a gym.

Whatever level of exercise is right for you, try to set realistic expectations for your progress. Remember, Rome wasn't built in a day. Be successful one day at a time. Be flexible. On a day when you come home from the office beat, you may only want to go for a walk rather than do aerobic cycling and lifting weights.

A Plan

Many people find it helpful to devise a personal exercise plan. If you haven't exercised regularly for some time, you'll need a do-able start-up. After your fitness level improves in time, you'll want to consider how to build upon your successes. If you set your original goals too high or too low, you may need to come up with an alternate plan and make some adjustments.

Perhaps you are reentering the world of regular exercise, and you devise a plan that begins with a commitment to take a brisk hour-long walk three times a week. After your body begins to adjust to this activity, you decide to add bike riding, and then you begin to incorporate some mild weight lifting with dumbbells. Increase your exercise regimen incrementally.

See a Doctor

A man who hasn't exercised regularly in several months or years should never begin an exercise program without first consulting with his doctor. Your doctor may want you to come in for a complete physical. If you have any specific chronic health problems, be sure to remind your physician of them.

Good Shoes

Fitness experts say that poor quality or poorly fitting shoes can take the fun out of exercise and may contribute to injuries. Go to any reputable athletic shoe chain store in your city and find a salesperson who is knowledgeable to help fit you with a good pair of shoes. You need shoes that support the arches and pad your impact to protect joints and grip ankles for lateral stability.

Start Slowly

If you're just beginning an exercise program, start out slowly. Those muscles haven't been worked for a long time and you don't want to overdo it. Perhaps a brisk one-mile walk four times a week might be enough for a while. Listen to your body. It will often tell you when it's okay to move on. Cramping and shin splints will let you know that you may be moving too quickly to the next level of exercise.

Join a Club or Go It Alone?

Most health clubs, which can be found in just about every community, are staffed by well-trained and knowledgeable fitness instructors who design an individual exercise program for each member. Perhaps you may want to consider joining a health club in your city. If you like to go it alone (or if you can't afford the club dues), this may not be an option to pursue. If you're undecided about joining a fitness club, you could sign up for a month or two to see if you like the "club scene."

Hardware

If you don't live in a region of the country that is warm throughout the year, you may want to consider buying exercise equipment. There are a large variety of effective exercisers from which to choose.

If you do decide to buy a piece of equipment, here's an important piece of advice: Try it out first! You can't know if you're going to like an exerciser unless you've had an opportunity to test it out. That's why it may not be the best idea to buy one over the phone—after watching an infomercial.

I have purchased many exercise devices over the years, and I can attest to the truth of the old adage "You get what you pay for." The cheaper machines generally don't deliver what you need and they usually don't last long.

Weight Training

While aerobic exercise is generally regarded as the best form of exercise for promoting overall health, there are many benefits to weight training. Health experts say lifting weights helps burn up excess stores of fat in the body and builds strength in the muscles. You might want to start with some simple exercises for your arm and shoulder muscles using twenty-five-pound weights. Weight training is an activity that usually requires some guidance—either from books you can find at your local library or from a qualified fitness instructor.

Schedule

With any type of exercise regimen, it's important to schedule the time. This is helpful because it makes exercise become a regular part of your daily routine. Many of us have found that it's better to have a regular exercise time established so that we don't find other things to do that divert us from our walk, jog, or exercise-machine workout.

Let your family members and friends know that this is a very important time for you and that you have committed yourself to exercise for a specific period of time. You might want to occasionally invite your wife or children along for your walk or run to give them a better appreciation of why your exercise time is important to you.

Extra Exercise

Along with planned and scheduled exercise periods, don't miss out on opportunities for additional exercise when you're going about the activities of day-to-day living. You may want to consider:

- Taking the steps instead of an elevator in an office building, department store, parking garage, or motel;
- Parking some distance from your place of employment to give yourself a little more space to cover and walk briskly to and from the office;
- Taking a brisk walk through a shopping mall before you begin to do your shopping;
- Using your coffee break during a workday to go for a walk outside the office. This daily habit can clear the mind and help restore energy for the remainder of the day.

Warm-up, Cool-Down

Fitness experts say there are three stages of exercise: the warm-up, the endurance stage, and the cool-down. They say the warm-up period, which often involves various stretching exercises, should last about five minutes. After at least thirty minutes in the endurance stage—the actual time of aerobic exercising—the cooling-off stage should last for another five or six minutes. This can involve walking and doing various stretching exercises that you used during the warm-up stage.[3] You might want to check out your local library for more details on the stages of exercise.

Split Workouts

In the past, health experts have said that pumping your heart and lungs for twenty minutes or more in one exercise session is the only way to get good aerobic exercise.

But some recent studies have indicated that many of the benefits of aerobic exercise can be gained by exercising in shorter workouts. Some fitness experts suggest that if you exercise ten minutes now, then save another ten-minute workout for later in the day, you'll gain almost as much from the two mini workouts as from one longer exercise session.

Boredom

Boredom can become a major detriment to achieving exercise objectives, say the fitness experts. For this reason, you may want to add some variety to your workout, perhaps experimenting with some different exercise machines and/or activities.

You might want to switch activities multiple times during a workout, mix your indoor training with outdoor exercise, and perhaps plan an easier workout on days when you feel tired or are having trouble pushing your motivational button.

Just Do It!

A regular exercise regimen will certainly *add to*, not *detract from*, your enjoyment of life. It's a great feeling to finish up an exercise session and know that you've accomplished something that will have long-lasting physical and psychological benefits.

Now, are you ready to make that trip to the sporting goods store?

For Thought and Discussion

1. What would you like to accomplish? Do you want to run in marathons, or do you simply want to get into better shape and improve your overall health?
2. Would you do better in a health club setting—with individualized instruction—or are you the type of person who would rather exercise on your own?
3. What could you do during your workday to get some extra exercise?
4. Realistically assess your current state of health—your age, your schedule, and other pertinent factors. Then devise your own exercise plan.

Notes

1. Michael van Straten, N.D., D.O., *The Complete Natural Health Consultant* (New York: Prentice Hall Press, 1987), 38.
2. Dr. Charles Serritella, *The Best of Total Health* (Ventura, Calif.: Regal Books, 1982), 143–144.
3. *The Complete Natural Health Consultant*, 40.

Healthy Relationships

Ringo Starr, the former Beatles drummer, was once asked what he enjoyed most about being a member of the world's most successful rock band. Starr told the interviewer that he certainly enjoyed the fame, adulation, and financial rewards. But, he said, as much as anything, he cherished his friendships with John, Paul, and George and the closeness they shared. Though these "lads from Liverpool" have had their ups and downs, the three surviving Beatles have told news reporters that they are close friends once again as they begin to enter the sunset years of their lives.

Professional athletes often say that their individual goals pale in comparison to their team goals. They say that working cooperatively with other men to reach a common goal is what motivates them—sometimes even more so than money. In this era of multimillion-dollar contracts, this is quite a statement!

Whose Team Are You On?/
Who Is on Your Team?

Men need to have vital, health-promoting relationships with other human beings—especially with other men. While our wife and children meet many of our needs for companionship, socialization, and emotional intimacy, there are other needs that can be met only through meaningful relationships with other men.

- We need to have a sense that we are not alone in this world—that we have friends on whom we can depend, and who have proven themselves to be trustworthy and reliable.
- We need to confide in someone besides our wife and family members. Sometimes family members are too close to the problem to give us a helpful, objective perspective. It's too much to ask of one person—even if it is a spouse—to be the only person we feel safe confiding in about matters of the heart and soul.
- We need to be accountable to Christian brothers in the Lord who will care enough to be honest with us about what they see in our lives.
- It's important to have friends who share a hobby or an interest—whether it's fishing, stamp collecting, going to baseball games, or writing and performing music. Sometimes we simply need a friend with whom we can have fun.
- Our families can benefit from having another Christian man as a friend of the family, a byproduct of our having a Christian friend.

Many Christian men would say that having a trusted male friend is very important. But how many men have a relationship like this? Many men are so pressed for time that they feel a friendship could never be a priority in their lives. Some have told me that all their needs for closeness, emotional support, and companionship are met by their family members. And, quite tragically, some men have said their wives are so jealous of their time and attention that they don't allow their husbands the "luxury" of having friendships with other men.

Other men I've talked with about this subject admit to being reluctant to allow a relationship with another man to transcend the superficial. They may have a fear of becoming open and honest with another man because they've been ignored, abused, or in competition with men all of their lives. Many of us feel that openness or vulnerability is a major character flaw in a man. Small wonder so many men today have had problems with alcohol and substance abuse.

Maybe you're thinking, *I already have some friends.* But do your friends really *know* you? Do you have friends who will listen to you when you need to talk, or offer you support and encouragement when you're grappling with a major problem?

Men who connect with each other solely on the basis of a shared male interest—such as hunting or fishing, following a sports team, or having coffee and a doughnut at the local diner—will be doomed to having superficial friendships that don't meet an innermost need for intimacy and companionship.

A few years ago an elderly man shared with me that a friend of his had committed suicide only a few weeks prior to our conversation. Bob and his friend spent a lot of time in a local men's social club. One night Bob was awakened by someone calling to tell him that his friend had killed himself.

"His doctor told him six months before that he had terminal cancer," Bob explained, tears welling in his eyes. "But he hadn't said a word about it to me or anyone else at the club, as far as I know. He left a note saying he killed himself because he didn't want to go through a lot of pain. I wish I would have known. Maybe I could have helped him in some way."

Bob's friend had carried his secret with him for several months without the support and encouragement true friends could have provided during his last days on earth. Sadly, he decided to die alone.

Building a Team

Like anything else that's important in life, having healthy friendships involves a commitment of time and a certain amount of effort. What do you get in return?

- Someone who will stand with you during the rough times and celebrate with you and share in the good times,
- Someone who can offer good advice and counsel,
- Someone to give a helping hand when needed,
- Someone who will hold you accountable,
- Someone who can become a friend to your family.

One close friend is great, but having a team of friends—who have various life skills—is even better! A man is truly blessed who has a number of friends who know the ropes in a variety of areas, such as marriage, work, finances, and raising children.

Dave gets together with Jerry and his family for ball games and an occasional camping trip. This is a time for the two men to blow off steam and have some fun. Dave meets with Lou biweekly to pray and talk more openly. While Jerry is more or less Dave's peer, Lou is older and has experienced a lot of life. He has more insight and more spiritual wisdom. Dave's friend Bill is a guy who really knows finances and investing and offers Dave some practical advice about how to better manage his family budget.

Ken is a person who is not as outgoing as Dave. He's also undergoing a very stressful period in his job. He relies a lot on one friend, Mark, for openness, advice, and an occasional hunting trip. While Ken is benefiting from his friendship with Mark, he hasn't yet connected with other men who have a variety of giftings and areas of expertise.

Building a web of connectedness with other men leads to emotional and spiritual (even physical) health. The self-made-man syndrome is a formula for missing out on life. Even if it feels risky to make friends, you'll find that the risk is most often well worth taking. When you develop a relationship with a man that blossoms into a lifelong friendship, you have added something very valuable to your life.

Some financial experts advise clients that it is a good idea to diversify their economic investments. You may want to diversify in the area of relationships. Many of us benefit from having friends who come from a variety of backgrounds and who have differing personality traits.

Let's take a look at a few of the personality types you might want to include in your web of healthy relationships:

1. *Lighthearted, fun-loving people.* It is great to have some friends to meet with for the primary purpose of enjoying leisure time, having a few laughs, and generally enjoying one another's company.

2. *Avant-garde, nonconformist types.* These are the folks who are a trifle eccentric and maybe have some really different opinions and interests, but they are usually colorful and fascinating to be around.

3. *Practical, down-to-earth types.* If you want some good advice on when to plant rutabagas, for instance, look to these people. They will be able to tell you the best paint to use on your house, some tried and true strategies for disciplining your kids, and maybe even give you some financial pointers.

4. *Deep thinkers and philosophers.* These are the friends you will want to seek out when you want to explore deep spiritual truths, share your innermost feelings, and/or get some advice when you are treading rough waters.

What other personality types might be represented in your list of friends?

How to Begin

To pave the way for sharing your innermost thoughts and feelings, it often helps to explain to another person the path you've walked leading up to the time of your meeting. This helps the other person understand the emotional baggage you've had to carry into adulthood because of the psychological woundings most of us have sustained (to varying degrees) in childhood.

Developing trust between two people—even if they are Christians—takes some time and a commitment to the relationship. If you want to have friends you can count on through thick and thin, you must prove yourself dependable and trustworthy.

All friendships—especially deep-level friendships—need to be proven safe. Here are some factors that help make for good, safe relationships:

Reliability. We need to be able to count on our friends through thick and thin.

Confidentiality. We need to know that we can speak to our friends about personal matters and that these comments will be kept confidential.

Respect. We need to have friends who treat us with dignity and respect.

Compassionate honesty. We need friends who will be honest with us; mixing honesty with compassion so that we don't feel judged or condemned.

A Friend Should Help You Become a Better Man

The authors of *Worry-Free Living* say,[1]

> Not all friendships are healthy. Some can actually *cause* anxiety instead of relieve it. If you feel some doubt as to whether or not a relationship is positive, ask yourself this question: "Is this friendship developing me?"
>
> If the relationship is one-way, with one partner al-

ways giving and the other always receiving, the answer is probably no. If it is a dependency relationship in which one person feels slighted if (he) isn't in (his) friend's company every day, the answer is no.

If it is a fair-weather relationship that withers when one of the partners endures a period of adversity, the answer is no. If it is an ego-boosting relationship in which one person merely strokes the ego of the other person without giving honest—even negative—feedback, the answer is no.

Just as happiness and forgiveness are choices, so is friendship. Each of us has to choose to develop friendships, and each of us must decide what kind of and how many friends we want.

A Question of Balance

Healthy relationships must also be balanced relationships. Good friendships are based on a healthy give-and-take between two people that I liken to riding on a seesaw at a neighborhood park. Sometimes a friend is down, defeated, and dejected. If I'm on the up side of the seesaw, I can help lift my friend off the ground by listening to him, supporting him, and encouraging him.

Other times I may be the one on the down end of life's proverbial seesaw, and I will need some support and encouragement from a friend to help me get my posterior up off the gravel. If the friendship is unbalanced, where one person is always in need and the other is always meeting those needs, the relationship is unhealthy.

Another way that a relationship can become unbalanced is if two people are at significantly different stages of growth and development as individuals and as Christians.

When I was in my late thirties, I developed a number of relationships based on leading men to a salvation experience and on discipling and counseling younger Christian men.

These friendships were very important to the young men I counseled and discipled, but I had a void in my own life. There were very few more spiritually mature Christian men I could turn to when I needed advice, counsel, and someone to stand with me through the hard times I was experiencing.

When I tried to obtain this kind of spiritual and emotional support and encouragement from a few of the young men I was discipling, I was often disappointed. Since I had established many relationships based upon my role as a teacher and encourager, these young men seemed reluctant to participate in a role reversal.

While it is important to cultivate relationships with men in varying stages of spiritual and emotional growth and development, I think it is very important that at least some of those men are on somewhat equal footing. I also believe that it's a tremendous asset to have at least one older Christian man as a friend. I seek out these seasoned Christian brothers because I know I will benefit from their wisdom and experience.

Boundary Issues in Friendships

Over the years I've run into some problems in relationships based upon boundary issues. If you're old enough to remember the youth culture of the 1960s, you've probably heard the phrase "I need my space." We all need some space, and boundaries are our space. They provide us with a sense of physical and emotional self-protection.

Let me give you a very blatant example of one man crossing another man's boundaries:

John visits Mike for the first time. As soon as John comes through the door, he walks into the kitchen and opens the refrigerator. "Don't you have any soda pop?" he asks Mike. Then they walk into the living room and John sees Mike's saxophone standing in a corner. Without asking, John opens the case, removes the horn, and begins to blow into the mouthpiece. In only a few moments, John has crossed boundaries twice. Those two trespasses are enough to make Mike decide he'll never invite John into his home again.

Other forms of boundary crossing can be much more subtle and less recognizable. But most of us can sense when our boundaries are being crossed—either physically or emotionally.

Since I don't like to have my boundaries crossed, I try to do my best not to step over another person's boundaries. Perhaps you see something in your friend's life that causes you concern. You don't want to see your friend stumble but neither do you want him to feel that his boundaries are being crossed. What do you do?

Often it's better not to say or do anything. You may simply decide to put your friend's problem into the Lord's hands. Sometimes you'll need to wait patiently until your friend is ready to discuss his problem—when he is ready to approach you about it. But if you are quick to the draw about pointing out problems you see in other people's lives, you'll likely find yourself wondering why you can't keep any friends.

Many years ago a close friend of mine—we'll call him Tim—became engaged to a woman I'd known for some time and who had many admirable qualities. But when I saw the two young people together on several occasions, I knew something was missing in their relationship. They were both Christians, they were compatible, and they had fun together, but it was obvious to me that they weren't in love. I prayed for Tim and his fiancée and asked God to intervene if they were on the verge of making a big mistake.

As wedding plans were being made, I became increasingly convinced that Tim and his fiancée were headed for major heartache. But I'd kept my thoughts to myself until one day when Tim and I were making a short car trip together. Out of the blue, Tim said something like, "Jim, I'm feeling that something isn't right between me and [his fiancée]. I can't really put my finger on it, but there seems to be something missing in our relationship. What do you think?"

Since Tim had invited me to share my thoughts, I told him that I had serious misgivings about his impending marriage. I explained to him that, as his friend, I had to be honest in suggesting that he reconsider whether or not God intended that he and this woman walk to the altar together.

Although he wasn't especially happy about hearing what I had to say—actually, he was somewhat angry with me—Tim knew that I wasn't overstepping his boundaries by telling him this. After all, he'd asked for my opinion.

Tim and his fiancée never did make it to the altar. They eventually each married other people and those marriages have lasted for many years. On occasion, Tim and I will talk about the marriage that wasn't to be, and he'll thank me for caring enough about him to help him face the truth.

What made this a very positive incident in our friendship was that I had waited until Tim approached me before I offered my opinion about his impending marriage. Believe me, I had to bite my tongue many times to keep from offering advice prematurely.

Another friend and I were recently discussing boundary issues in a relationship when he said something that I thought was particularly insightful.

"When I feel the most out of control with my life," he said, "that's when I'm inclined to want to try to control someone else's life."

We should resist every impulse to try to fix a friend's problems and also be wary of someone who repeatedly tries to fix ours. If the other person can't accept your need to have physical and emotional boundaries, the relationship is likely doomed to failure.

Unrealistic Expectations

Another way to destroy a fledgling relationship with another man is to expect your friend to be perfect. We need to accept each other's individual differences and imperfections and realize that we aren't God's cookie-cutter creations. I often remind my friends and acquaintances that they'll be sorely disappointed if they expect me to be unwaveringly consistent in my dealings with them. The only man to walk the planet who was always consistent and perfect was our Lord Jesus Christ.

There are times when I don't completely understand why a Christian brother has a weakness in a particular area of his life, but that's to be understood, since I haven't walked in his shoes for forty some years either. That's where the concept of grace comes into the picture. If we tend to judge one another by the law, we'll all be in trouble. But if we try to practice extending grace and mercy to each other, our relationships will be fruitful.

Bill was supposed to be at Aaron's house for supper at six. Aaron's wife had spent all afternoon in the kitchen fixing a special meal for Bill, who is a young single man. But at six-thirty Bill has still not arrived. Aaron phones Bill's apartment, and a groggy voice answers, "Oh, no! I worked the night shift last night and set my alarm for four-thirty. I must have slept through it!"

Aaron can choose to be angry with Bill and not invite him over for supper again, or he can chuckle and admit that he has slept through an alarm before, too, and missed an appointment. The first response is based on the law, the second is based on grace and mercy. One response ends a relationship and the other extends it.

Some Christian men I've known tend to easily write off a friend once the relationship becomes a little sticky or complicated—or when they see some glaring imperfection or flaw in their Christian brother. I've found over the years that when a person becomes difficult, it's often his way of letting you know that he's going through a time of hardship and struggle. Though my first inclination is to want to withdraw, that's not the response God wants from me. I need to make it known that I'm willing to listen and that I'm willing to help in any way I can.

Real Friends Are in It for Keeps

It's not an easy task to make a new friend, and it can be even more difficult to remain friends for many years. In some ways, friendships are like a marriage relationship. Though there are times of stress and difficulty, a marriage will survive if both the husband and wife are committed to their relationship for the long haul. True friends are in it for keeps. They're committed to the relationship and are unwilling to let petty grievances and grudges destroy something that God has intended for good in their lives.

I don't know about you, but I want to be the kind of friend who is described in the seventeenth chapter of the book of Proverbs: "A friend loves at all times, and a brother is born for adversity" (v. 17).

Though the world would have you believe that all relationships are tenuous and fleeting, Christian friends can indeed be friends forever.

For Thought and Discussion

1. Do you ever feel alone and isolated, even though you have a wife and children? Do you believe it is important to have male Christian friends?

2. Is it difficult for you to get past the superficial when you interact with other men? How can someone make you feel more comfortable about sharing your thoughts and feelings? What can you do to make another person feel more comfortable sharing on a deeper level with you?

3. What are the barriers standing in your way of developing healthy relationships with other Christians? How can you overcome them?

4. Are you willing to remain committed to a friend even if the relationship becomes difficult?

5. Do you understand the importance of the concept of boundaries in a friendship?

Notes

1. Frank Minirth, M.D., Paul Meier, M.D., Don Hawkins, Th.M., *Worry-Free Living* (Nashville, Tenn.: Thomas Nelson Publishers, 1989), 151–152.

Wounds That Can't Be Hidden

A television documentary crew took a group of '90s teenagers into a room to watch old television programs from the '50s and '60s. The TV folks wanted to see how offspring of baby boomers would react to these programs from a bygone era.

I was interested in seeing how the kids would react, too. Since I'm a baby boomer, these were the television programs I grew up watching. I don't know what the TV producers expected, but I anticipated the kids would be hooting and howling five minutes into the first episode of *Leave It to Beaver*.

The End of Innocence

Boy, did I get a surprise! The '90s teenagers didn't laugh. Quite the opposite. They seemed mesmerized by what they saw, eyes glued to the screen. These images were transporting them to a different world—a world where moms wore aprons, baked cookies, and cooked supper, and dads arrived home precisely at 5:10 P.M., changed clothes, and emerged in cardigan sweaters, casual slacks, and slippers. This was a world in which a young man's biggest challenge for the week might be deciding who to ask out for the Friday night teen dance.

The '90s kids lamented how much our American culture has changed in the last thirty years. Beaver and his buddies traded baseball cards and spent Saturday mornings in the local soda shop. Many children of the '90s dodge bullets going to school and come home in the afternoon to an empty house, or to parents who smoke marijuana and snort cocaine in front of the TV. Even Christian kids find that hectic schedules and career demands keep parents away from the home and a real family life together.

"Secret" Sins of Our Parents

It's discomforting to think of the psychological and behavioral problems the children of the '90s are going to carry with them through the rest of their lives because of parents who were preoccupied with drug parties, illicit affairs, and illustrious careers. I worry about what the future will hold for all of us as these emotionally wounded kids of the boomers grow into adulthood.

If I had been a part of the discussion taking place after the teens viewed the old movies and sitcoms for the TV documentary, I could have said some things that probably would have surprised those young people.

Though I grew up during the era that those TV programs were supposed to reflect, my childhood wasn't anything like what the teens were seeing on the big screen. The same could probably be said about many adults who grew up during the '50s and '60s. Many of us in the baby boomer generation had parents who were divorced, who were substance abusers (mostly alcohol back then), and who were involved in extra-marital affairs.

The main difference between the '60s and the '90s is that our modern culture tends to flaunt its sin and celebrate a way of life devoid of morals and ethics. The baby boomers' parents were more discreet. In those days, appearances were important. Many families gave the impression that they had it all together, but there were many secrets and hidden sins. All that glittered was not gold in the golden years of innocence prior to Vietnam and the emergence of the Woodstock generation.

Admitting that you had an emotional or mental health problem during that era was taboo. These problems were denied and kept from public view and knowledge. I heard a comedian say that the only way a man could get help from a mental health professional back then was if he was discovered wandering naked around his neighbor's yard, carrying a hatchet!

Healing Past Wounds Takes Time and Patience

Though our culture has become a bit more enlightened about mental and emotional illness, it doesn't mean people are actually being cured of these afflictions. Modern medicine and psychological therapies may have helped lessen symptoms in many people, but the root causes often remain.

If we'd all had *Leave It to Beaver* childhoods, we wouldn't be carrying so much baggage into adulthood. But some of us will be dealing with childhood wounds and hurts for the rest of our adult lives. Some Christians have told me that God has given them complete and almost instantaneous deliverance from past hurts and woundings (and I believe them). But for most of us, deliverance from the past is an ongoing process. I call it "progressive deliverance."

When a child is born, his or her mind is like a computer disk. Every experience the child has is stored on his or her internal disk and remains there for a lifetime as a subconscious memory. Though as adults we're often unaware of it, this disk is playing and replaying events from the past night and day. This is why it is possible to feel free-floating anxiety, depression, and anger without being able to put a finger on why we're having these feelings.

It's important that we come to understand how significant a role the past plays in our day-to-day emotional health and well-being. Subconscious memories from the past can cause major pain and trauma in the present.

A man we'll call Jeff is an example of how his can happen. Though the first few years of his life were normal by most standards, Jeff's life was turned upside down by events that occurred in his family beginning when he was about twelve years old. Without warning, at least to the children, Jeff's mother suddenly suffered a mental breakdown and was hospitalized. His mother's condition deteriorated until she was eventually admitted to a mental institution for long-term confinement.

This situation placed enormous stress and strain on Jeff's father, a business executive who had acquired some emotional scars of his own while serving overseas in combat during World War II. Though Jeff's father drank only moderately prior to his wife's breakdown, he soon began to drink heavily.

Jeff's older brother escaped the family turmoil by joining the U.S. Air Force. Being second oldest, responsibility for the two younger siblings fell to Jeff. He was only thirteen. The work and worry and stress of the situation went on for the next five years, until Jeff left for college 150 miles away. His leaving forced his father to take over the responsibility he'd abandoned for so many years.

Jeff graduated from college and went on to begin his career. Things seemed to be going fairly well for him as he neared his mid-twenties, but he often felt a vague sense of uneasiness and insecurity. During his late twenties, the "chickens" from Jeff's past "came to roost." He began to have panic attacks and unrelenting anxiety.

His doctor convinced him he should see a mental health counselor. Jeff had become a Christian several years before, but he couldn't find a Christian therapist in his town, so he went to one referred to him by the local mental health agency. This man reviewed Jeff's background and helped him to understand how his problems had their origin in the events of his childhood. Besides feeling overwhelmed due to the enormous responsibilities placed upon him at an early age, Jeff's subconscious thoughts revealed he'd felt abandoned by both his mother and father.

Though the therapist helped Jeff to understand *why* he was feeling the way he felt, leaving God out of the process delayed Jeff's emotional healing. Still battling anxiety, Jeff found a Christian counselor forty miles from his hometown. He needed more than an understanding of why he felt the way he did. He wanted to be *free* of these feelings—liberated from the soul-wrenching anxiety and insecurity he'd struggled with for years.

The Christian counselor also explored Jeff's childhood, but then she showed him how God could heal his emotional wounds. This process involved Jeff's exploring what the Scriptures have to say about God's relationship with His children as a loving Father. It also required allowing the Holy Spirit to do some supernatural healing, helping Jeff to experience God's love in the deeper recesses of his innermost heart and soul. Jeff also learned that he had to forgive his parents for "abandoning" him and for placing so much responsibility on him at an early age.

For the most part, Jeff is now free from the torment of anxiety and emotional insecurity. When he senses these feelings arising—often during a time of stress or change—he reflects on the love God has for him and reminds himself that he doesn't have to let his emotions be controlled by events of the past.

Perhaps your childhood was much less difficult than Jeff's, but you feel there are events from your past that are influencing your life today. Do you have unexplained feelings of anxiety, depression, and/or anger? Do you wonder why you're having these feelings or where they are coming from?

To acknowledge the influence events from your past may have on you today doesn't mean that you have to live in the past. But understanding how the past has affected you is important because it helps you to challenge unhealthy belief systems in your adult life.

Changing the Way We Perceive Events

What is a belief system? Let's consider the story of "Ted." At age ten he was sexually molested by a Scout leader during a campout. Because of this traumatic experience, Ted has trouble trusting men. As an adult, he doesn't have any male friends because his experience as a child led him to believe that he could be victimized again. Ted has established a belief system about all men based on his experience with one man twenty-five years ago.

To be able to have normal relationships with other men, Ted has to come to an understanding of how his childhood experience has influenced him as an adult. Then he has to challenge his beliefs: *Just because one man abused me when I was a child doesn't mean I have to fear* all *men as an adult.* He can also challenge this unhealthy belief system by reminding himself that he was an innocent child who was taken advantage of by an adult authority figure that he trusted. Now, at age thirty-five, he knows he would be better equipped to handle another adult male's sexual advances.

Most non-Christian psychotherapy takes a person through the process of understanding the past and challenging unhealthy belief systems. But that's where they leave you standing—a mile from the finish line. Ultimately, to be free from the influences of the past requires a third step—allowing God to do supernatural "surgery" in your heart and soul. That process is accomplished when a man is ready to open his heart to God and to allow Him to heal his hurts from the past and reprogram the computer disk of his mind.

Many of us find that we need to reexamine our concepts about who God really is and how He feels about us. A man who is a son of a demanding and hypercritical father will often find it difficult to view God as a Father in heaven who offers him unconditional love and acceptance.

The Bible is full of passages that reveal the depth of God's love for His children. One of my favorites is in the twenty-ninth chapter of the book of Jeremiah:

> "For I know the plans I have for you," declares the Lord, "plans to prosper you and not to harm you, plans to give you hope and a future" (v. 11).

Before I could be set free from my past, I had to gain a true revelation of the fact that God is on my side—that He wants the best for me and that He loves me in spite of all of my flaws and imperfections. Fifty years of Freudian-based psychotherapy can't come close to producing the inner healing that takes place when a human being actually begins to comprehend the depth of God's love for him. He is a loving and nurturing Father who is so concerned about His children that He's numbered the very hairs on our heads! (Matthew 10:30–31).

When we remember past hurts, we need to remind ourselves who we are as children of the Creator of the universe, people for whom God has a special purpose and plan.

Sometimes We Need a Helping Hand

Not everyone will need Christian counseling to be delivered from the pain of the past. But many people find it helpful. If you decide to work with a Christian counselor, go through the following checklist:

1. *Find a therapist you can trust.* Ask him or her for multiple references and make some phone calls on your own. Make sure you find a therapist who makes it easy for you to share your feelings, one who is not judging or condemning.

2. *Discuss your goals.* Work out a therapy contract that specifies what you hope to accomplish.

3. *Commit yourself to telling the whole truth.* Avoid posturing or making an effort to get the therapist to like you.

4. *Consider bringing your spouse in with you at some point in the process.* Your spouse needs to know about the issues you are confronting because they affect her as well, whether directly or indirectly.

5. *Make certain the therapy is producing good fruit in your life.* If this isn't happening, consider making a change.

6. *You may reach a point where a support group will better meet your needs.* Don't be afraid to suggest this to your counselor and ask him or her to refer you to a good group.

Some Pain, a Lot of Gain

Delving into the past to understand why you react as you do in the present can be difficult and painful. But the rewards far outweigh the discomforts. You have the opportunity to turn your emotional trials into gold.

Going through an emotional and spiritual restoration process is something like having a tooth pulled that has bothered you for a long time or a surgery done that improves your health and well-being. The procedures may hurt initially, but when they are done, real healing can begin.

Experiencing healing and deliverance from emotional wounds of the past will bring about tremendous rewards in your life in terms of peace and contentment. You will be healthier and happier both spiritually and physically. You will be a better husband, a better father, and a better friend. It could also open up a ministry for you. When you see others who are hurting, you will be better equipped to provide them with the support and encouragement they need.

Some Self-Therapy Suggestions

Not everyone is going to need the assistance of a Christian counselor or therapist. Sometimes having a bad day, whether because of present circumstances or events in the past, can afford us opportunity to practice self therapy. Following are some practical tips for the times when you feel a bit overwhelmed and you suspect that past traumas may be affecting your present state of mind.

1. *Be kind to yourself.* Do something relaxing alone or with your family. See a movie. Read a good book. Relax with a magazine or good music. Take in a sports event with a friend, take your kids to a park and play ball with them, or simply go for a walk.

2. *Meditate on the Word of God.* I don't mean here that you need to get into some arduous in-depth study. Rather, find some portions of Scripture that speak to you of God's deep love for His children. In a peaceful and quiet place, meditate on the Word and let the truth of God sink into your spirit.

3. *Talk to a close friend.* Unfortunately, not every Christian man is going to be able to tell someone else how he is feeling. But make an effort. Approach a friend who knows you well, one who will listen to you with compassion and

understanding. Seek out someone with similar life experiences to yours.

4. *Rest in the arms of your Father.* Allow God to impart to you His comfort and restoration. True rest and security is found under the shadow of His wings. Let the healing waters of His presence bathe you in love, acceptance, and a revelation of His perfect peace. Part of prayer is simply being in His presence and waiting on Him.

For Thought and Discussion

1. What events from your past may be causing you emotional discomfort in the present?
2. How do you handle feelings of anxiety, anger, and/or depression? Do you discuss how you are feeling with other people, or do you tend to clam up?
3. Do you believe that conventional sectarian psychotherapy has proven effective in helping people with emotional problems to fully recover? How does a Christian counselor differ in his or her approach?
4. Do you have a true personal revelation of God as a loving Father who offers unconditional love and acceptance, or do you find yourself trying to prove to God that you are worthy of being loved?

Some "Health Insurance" From Supplements

Your wife keeps telling you that you need to take a daily vitamin and mineral supplement, but you laugh it off. "I'm not one of those paranoid types," you say. "Let the health-crazed crowd deal with all that supplemental stuff. I'll get what I need from real food."

Like you, some health authorities believe that taking vitamins and other dietary supplements is a waste of time. They argue that the average person obtains all of the vitamins he or she needs by eating the right foods in the proper amounts.

In the other camp, however, are health professionals who believe that taking dietary supplements is almost a necessity in this era of fast-food meals, stress, and environmental toxins. And most of these people aren't New Agers or eccentrics; they're ordinary folks like you and me.

So who's right? That's for you to decide for yourself. But I align myself with those who believe vitamins, minerals, and other dietary supplements are necessary to ensure good health as we near the twenty-first century.

Why Take Dietary Supplements?

Millions of Americans take dietary supplements. Physicians often prescribe them, but most consumers tend to buy them without a doctor's recommendation. Here are only a few of the reasons why:

1. Healthy intakes of calcium and vitamin D help build bones and keep them strong.

2. At least four nutrients—beta-carotene, vitamins C and E, and selenium—may guard against cancer and reduce your chances of developing this disease.

3. Certain vitamins may affect important brain chemicals, influencing the quality of your sleep, your mood, and other aspects of your mental outlook and of your overall sense of well-being.

There are scores of other reasons why many nutritionists believe that taking supplements is a smart practice, and I'll go into more specifics about them later in this chapter.

I tend to look at the practice as a form of "health insurance." I try to eat the right foods in the proper amounts to obtain the vitamins and minerals I need, but it's not always easy to eat a wide enough variety of foods on a consistent basis—even if you're nutrition conscious. Also, mineral-depleted soils tend to make our foods less nutritious than they were at one time. Stress, environmental, and life-style factors also rob our bodies of vital nutrients.

When I take a good vitamin and mineral supplement each day, I feel that I am giving my body the nutrients it needs to carry on effectively. These supplements are relatively inexpensive and can generally do no harm unless taken in absurdly high dosages. The way I look at it, I have everything to gain and very little to lose.

Deciding What Supplements to Take

What vitamins, minerals, and other dietary supplements should a man take each day?

Every person's nutritional needs are different. I do not sub-scribe to the one-size-fits-all concept when it comes to nutri-tion. Let me also say that nothing in this book should be in-terpreted as a diagnosis of an illness or a prescription for an ailment. Talk with your doctor about what dietary supple-ments you should take, and keep your personal physician aware of changes you decide to make.

Unfortunately, some medical doctors are not very well in-formed about dietary supplements. For that reason, I suggest you search out a physician who is knowledgeable about nu-trition and diet. If possible, find a Christian doctor who un-derstands God's natural plan for our health and who doesn't hesitate to seek God for guidance and direction.

Lately, I've become concerned that many people—includ-ing a large number of Christians—are selling dietary supple-ments without any knowledge of how they work. One woman at a church I once attended was selling herbal supplements by the case. I asked her if she knew what herbs were in the for-mulas and she said she had no idea. When I investigated, I found that her herbal weight-loss formula contained a natural stimulant that can cause emotional anxiety and elevate blood pressure.

Some people reason that if taking a recommended dose of a vitamin or mineral is healthy, why not take ten times that amount and gain even more health benefits? This can send you to the hospital. Taking massive doses of vitamins and minerals can be dangerous. Vitamins and minerals are, generally speak-ing, safe and devoid of side effects when taken in reasonable dosages. But they do have the potential to harm the body when taken in massive amounts.

An informed physician or nutritionist can tell you what is a safe dosage and what is not. Be especially careful about tak-ing herbal products. I believe God has provided us with herbs to help us stay healthy and to regain health, but some herbs have side effects. A few may be toxic to the liver when taken in large amounts. I'd advise you to find a reputable book about herbs and get some solid information before you decide to take any herbal product.

Use discernment about herbal formulas that don't specifically list the herbs contained in a capsule. Taking an herbal formula without knowing exactly what it contains is unwise and potentially dangerous—especially if you have any health problems connected with hypertension, heart disease, or liver function. Herbal supplements are becoming "big business," and sometimes dollar signs push the marketing of these products without regard to how they may affect the consumer's overall health.

I suggest that you do your own library research on vitamin and mineral supplements. *Earl Mindell's Vitamin Bible* lists specific vitamin and mineral uses for various health conditions and even breaks down its recommendations by job circumstances—such as for people who work at night.[1]

There are many other books on the market about taking vitamin and mineral supplements that are well researched and instructive. One that will help you avoid overdosing on vitamins and minerals is called *The Right Dose: How to Take Vitamins and Minerals Safely.*[2]

Since many vitamins and minerals work together synergistically, I'm a firm believer in taking a multivitamin and mineral supplement. I make sure mine contains beta-carotene, vitamins A, B1, B2, niacin, B6, folic acid, B12, biotin, PABA, choline, pantothenic acid, inositol, and vitamins C, D, and E. Also, the minerals calcium, magnesium, phosphorus, potassium, iron, copper, manganese, zinc, chromium, and selenium.

When you think in terms of buying a multivitamin and mineral supplement, you need to ask yourself how much you are willing to spend. In general, the more expensive health-food-store brand supplements are thought to be of higher quality than supplements purchased in your favorite discount store or drugstore. But, in my estimation, many of the cheaper brands will still do the job.

A Little Help for Your Digestive System

It doesn't do any good to take vitamins and minerals unless your body can digest them. For this reason, I buy a multivitamin and mineral supplement that comes in capsule form rather than a hard tablet. Some people believe that an even better way to ensure absorption of nutrients is to purchase powdered or liquid forms of vitamin and mineral supplements. If you buy a cheaper brand of any supplement, look for one that guarantees laboratory testing, assuring that it will dissolve relatively quickly in your body. This information can be found on the bottle or outer packaging.

To help with absorption of both food and supplements, I take digestive enzyme capsules. Digestive enzymes do the work of digesting proteins, carbohydrates, and fats in our bodies. Because they are extremely sensitive to heat, many experts believe most of the natural enzymes in our food are destroyed when foods are cooked or when they are improperly stored. If you eat a diet plentiful in raw, uncooked fruits and vegetables, you may be getting the enzymes you need from your diet.

For the vast majority of us who don't eat enough raw foods, digestive enzyme supplements are available. These come from animal or plant sources, and can make a big difference for you, especially if you suffer from chronic indigestion or diarrhea, as I did. My family doctor told me these were stress-related symptoms, but after taking digestive enzymes, my symptoms went away. These supplements can be purchased at health-food stores or through health-food mail order catalogues.

Along with the controversy about whether dietary supplements are really necessary, there is some disagreement about how much of these nutrients we really need to be healthy.

Rethinking the RDA standard

Many vitamin and mineral formulas that are sold in large discount stores and drugstores contain only the Recommended Daily Allowance (RDA) of vitamins and minerals. This guideline was instituted nearly half a century ago by the U.S. Food and Nutrition Board to determine daily amounts of vitamins and minerals needed to prevent disease.

But many health professionals, including well-respected physician Dr. James F. Balch, believe that the RDA is only the bare minimum of nutrients needed and that we should be taking in an Optimum Daily Allowance of nutrients to enhance our health. As I do, Dr. Balch believes that a vitamin and mineral program can be custom tailored to suit the needs of each individual.[3]

I'm not a megadoser when it comes to supplements but neither am I an RDAer. I tend to travel the middle of the road.

Vitamin C—a Power Supplement

Along with a good multivitamin and mineral supplement, I believe that almost everyone can benefit from taking additional vitamin C. Again, if you have any ongoing health problems or if you're taking a prescription medication, check first with a nutritionally aware physician. Vitamin C performs a number of important functions. Some of these include iron absorption, fighting infection, formation of brain chemicals, metabolism of other nutrients and proteins, and healing wounds. Many experts, including Nobel Prize-winning scientist Linus Pauling, believe that vitamin C supplementation can significantly strengthen the immune system.

Not long ago I heard a prominent television evangelist say that vitamin C supplements have boosted his immune response to the point where he seldom, if ever, gets a cold or flu during the winter months. He said he has found 2,000 mg. to be a protective daily dose of vitamin C for him.

Many multivitamin and mineral supplements found in discount stores and drugstores contain only 50 to 80 mg. of vitamin C. On the other extreme, some scientists and health experts suggest taking up to 10,000 mg. a day in divided doses. Again, I take the middle road. Along with my vitamin and mineral supplement, I take an additional 1,000 mg. of vitamin C. If I have a cold or the flu (or if I'm trying to protect myself against illness during the winter months), I sometimes increase that dosage to 2,000–4,000 mg. a day, but only for a relatively short period of time. If you are taking a vitamin C supplement, and your doctor has scheduled you for laboratory tests, tell your physician beforehand what you are taking. High doses of vitamin C can give false readings on some tests.[4]

The "Fountain of Youth" and Other Supplements

Two relatively new dietary supplements on the market break the mold in many ways when it comes to natural supplementation. These are not vitamins, minerals, or herbs, but hormones. Melatonin is the primary hormone released by the pineal gland. It is said to be an important factor in sleep, aging, breast cancer, and the immune system as a whole. Another very popular new product is called DHEA. This is a hormone produced by the adrenal glands. It is being touted as a fountain of youth that can restore some of the energy and stamina lost as human beings age.

My personal opinion about these two hot-selling products is that one should exercise great caution in using them. Because these supplements are hormones, they are not from food or plant sources as are vitamins, minerals, and herbs. While I have read studies in which researchers have proclaimed Melatonin and DHEA supplements to be safe, I believe the jury is still out on them and will be for many years. I want to see the long-term effects of taking these hormones before I become enthusiastic about them.

If you do decide to take DHEA or Melatonin, I strongly advise you to first consult with a nutritionally aware physician. Many doctors will test DHEA levels in the blood or saliva before giving a patient the go-ahead to take a DHEA supplement.

Herbs: God's Natural Medicines

While hormonal supplements have been on the market only a relatively short time, herbs have been sold and used for health purposes for thousands of years. Records from ancient civilizations including Roman, Egyptian, Persian, and Hebrew indicate that herbs have been used extensively to treat practically every illness and disorder known to man.[5]

I believe herbs are a truly wonderful gift that God has given us in His creation. Used with wisdom, herbs can accomplish, with fewer side effects and much less expense, many of the things prescription pharmaceutical drugs are intended to accomplish.

In light of this information, however, don't be an unenlightened herb user. I suggest visiting your local library or your health-food store book section to do some research before you begin taking any new herbal supplement.

There are hundreds of herbal products sold and they all have specific uses. Obviously, we cannot discuss every one of them in this chapter, but I will cover some of the more popular ones.

Garlic. If you're like me, you probably thought the only use for garlic was to season bread eaten with spaghetti. But garlic is a truly remarkable substance. It has been researched by a number of prominent scientists for its health-promoting qualities. Dr. Benjamin Lau, who has a medical degree as well as a Ph.D. in immunology, has done research leading to the conclusion that garlic can help prevent and even reverse cardiovascular disease. He also believes garlic has the potential to prevent and possibly cure certain types of cancer, enhance the body's immune system against allergies and other related disorders, and help the body deal with stress.[6] You can, of course, eat fresh garlic. But there are many garlic products—including capsules, tablets, and oils—that can be taken as a dietary supplement. Some of these products contain odor-modified garlic, so as not to be offensive on your breath or skin.

Echinacea. This herb is very popular during the winter cold-and-flu season. Echinacea has been found to help protect healthy cells in the body from viral and bacterial attack. Researchers say that echinacea stimulates activity of the immune system, affording us an extra layer of protection against various illnesses. My family's use of echinacea during the winter months—combined with a vitamin C supplement—has enabled us to significantly reduce the number of wintertime cold-and-flu episodes. We're believers in the immune-enhancing power of echinacea. Some herbalists contend that echinacea should be taken only during the months when colds and flus proliferate because they believe that the herb loses its effectiveness when taken daily over long stretches of time.

Saw Palmetto. This herbal supplement has proven to be very effective for many men. A few years ago I became extremely sick with a high fever, pain in my back and groin, and difficulty urinating. I went to an emergency room and was told that I had an infection of the prostate gland. The doctor on call told me prostate gland infections are very common in adult men. I took a course of antibiotics and it cleared up the infection. However, a few months later I got another infection. Then another one. For the next five months I had to take powerful antibiotics every day to keep the infection down. Then I happened to read an article written by a medical doctor about an herb useful against enlarged prostate conditions and prostate infections.

I bought some of the herb the doctor suggested—saw pal-

metto—and began taking it daily. Within days, my prostate infection cleared up and I haven't had any subsequent infections
for about a year. Saw palmetto is often sold as a part of prostate
health formulas that also contain zinc, a mineral many experts
believe is important to prostate gland health.

Ginseng. I can also vouch for the benefits of the herb ginseng. As I mentioned earlier in this book, I have adult-onset
diabetes that I have been able to control without insulin in-
jections. Several months ago I read that drinking ginseng tea
would help keep blood sugar levels under better control for
many diabetics. I have to admit that I was somewhat skeptical,
but I bought some, and after drinking it for one day I took my
blood sugar reading. I was shocked! My blood sugar level was
much lower that night than the night before. Since then, ginseng tea (along with drinking aloe-vera juice) has helped me
to maintain tighter control of my blood sugar levels. Another
benefit is that it gives me a boost of energy for several hours.

My younger brother is a respiratory therapist with a demanding job. He asked me recently what he could do to help
alleviate fatigue. I suggested that he try ginseng. He was
amazed at the energy boost he received from this remarkable
herb. In China and other countries, ginseng is considered to
be an overall tonic to maintain health and to help speed re-
covery from illness. I must say that some people have said ginseng made them a bit nervous and shaky when they first tried
it, but over time their bodies seemed to adjust to it.

Evening Primrose Oil. Some fantastic claims are made for
this oil that comes from the evening primrose flower. Many
scientists believe that evening primrose oil can help lower
blood pressure and blood cholesterol, aid in weight reduction,
and in the treatment of mild to moderate rheumatoid arthritis.
Many companies combine evening primrose oil with vitamin
E to protect it from the destructive effects of oxygen. Evening
primrose oil is a source of essential fatty acids that scientists

believe protect cells against invading viruses, bacteria, and allergies.

Ginkgo Biloba. This is an herb that has become increasingly popular, especially among senior citizens. Many scientists believe that within the leaves of the ginkgo tree is a substance that can be of tremendous help to older people with memory problems. Ginkgo biloba is said to improve blood flow to the brain. It has also been used by some physicians to treat irregular heartbeat.

St. John's Wort. Some nutritionally aware physicians believe this herb can often be as effective as prescription antidepressants for relieving mild to moderate depression. It is also used to help relieve anxiety and for relief of sciatica and neuralgia.

These are only a few of the hundreds of herbal supplements on the market. If you have an interest in herbs, again I would advise that you look into the function of each herb and its possible side effects. What works for one person may not work for another. That's why I've been willing to experiment with various herbs to find out which are beneficial for me. Many herbal products that have helped others have had no particular effect when I've taken them, while others have given good to excellent results.

You, too, may decide to do some experimenting with herbs. Make certain it is *enlightened* experimentation.

Beware of the "Snake Oil" Salesman

Because the sale of dietary supplements is a multimillion-dollar business enterprise, there are a few unscrupulous people out there who are modern-day versions of the "snake oil" salesman. Be skeptical of any product that claims to be a sure cure for a specific disease or disorder.

In recent years I've become concerned about nutritional

faddishness. I've known people who sell a particular dietary supplement or herbal product and claim that it is *the answer* for every illness and affliction known to man. Some of these products can be helpful, but they are more beneficial when taken in addition to other supplements and a well-rounded diet.

Let me give you a specific example to illustrate my point. In the small town where I live, there are countless numbers of people taking weight-loss supplements that contain the herb Ma huang. This plant, used in China for thousands of years as an antiasthmatic, contains ephedrine. In people who have high blood pressure or heart problems, ephedrine (a stimulant) can be dangerous. Also, people who are being treated with antidepressant medications should never take Ma huang.

Of all of the people I've talked with who have taken a weight-loss supplement containing Ma huang, I've *never* come across a person who was aware that this herb can have potentially life-threatening side effects. The person who sold it to them—often through a home business enterprise—hasn't educated the consumer about the product, and the consumer hasn't taken the time to research the product before taking it. That's plain foolishness on the part of both parties!

A few years ago, before I learned about the potential dangers of some herbal dietary supplements, I ordered a product containing Ma huang from a Christian company that sells herbal products. Near the end of the first day of taking the capsules, I began to notice some rather disturbing nervousness. I also felt very tense and somewhat hyper.

At the time, I was being treated for moderately high blood pressure. I took my blood pressure on my home monitor and it had climbed well out of the moderately high range into the seriously high range. I didn't take any more of the "natural diet pills." By the end of the next day the anxiety had left and my blood pressure had dropped to what was then its usual range.

Foods and Herbs Are God's Gifts to Humankind

I am grateful to God for the foods and herbs He's given us to help maintain our health. He is indeed the Creator of all life and He has given us everything we need to sustain our health for a lifetime.

When I was a small child, I'd often throw aside gifts I found under the Christmas tree until I found one that was fully assembled and ready to operate. Later I found that the gifts I'd discarded—the ones that took time and effort to assemble—became my most prized possessions in the weeks and months that followed.

To discover all of the health-sustaining properties in the natural gifts God has supplied us with, we sometimes need to do some homework to uncover nature's secrets. I've found this to be a fascinating and rewarding exploration. To know more about God's creation is to learn more about the Creator himself.

You, too, might want to set out on your own personal discovery quest.

For Thought and Discussion

1. Do you eat a wide enough variety of foods daily to get all of the vitamins and minerals you need?
2. Is your life particularly stressful and/or are you exposed to any environmental toxins? If so, do you believe these factors might deplete your body of essential vitamins and minerals?
3. Are you willing to do some reading on your own to learn about nutrients and herbs that might improve your health and the quality of your life?

Notes

1. Earl Mindell, *Earl Mindell's Vitamin Bible* (New York: Warner Books, Inc., 1991).
2. Patricia Hausman, M.S., *The Right Dose: How to Take Vitamins and Minerals Safely* (New York: Ballantine Books, 1992).
3. James F. Balch, M.D., and Phyllis A. Balch, C.N.C., *Prescription for Nutritional Healing* (Garden City Park, New York: Avery Publishing Group, 1990), 4.
4. Hausman, *The Right Dose*, 196.
5. Balch, *Prescription for Nutritional Healing*, 46.
6. Benjamin Lau, M.D., Ph.D., *Garlic for Health* (Wilmot, Wis.: Lotus Light Publications, 1988).

Turning Stress Into Strength

Steve is a man who works in a high-pressure sales job. He sometimes has migraine headaches and heart palpitations. Steve can't relax when he's away from work, and he can never really seem to get his mind off his job. At night he even dreams about problems at the office.

Larry is a husband and father. He's also had to become a parent to his own father, who is in the early stages of Alzheimer's disease. While trying to put away some money in his children's college fund, Larry is seeing his personal savings become depleted as he helps to pay for his father's care. At age forty-six, Larry wonders how he and his wife will ever survive financially after his retirement. Or will he ever really be in a position to retire?

Jason and his wife are newlyweds, having been married little more than a year. While the first few months of their marriage were idyllic in many ways, lately the couple has been arguing a lot. Jason's wife tells him that she thinks he often doesn't understand her and that he doesn't know how to communicate with her. Jason, who was raised in a home where feelings weren't shared and articulated, can't comprehend what his young wife wants from him. He's often left shaking his head when she says she is frustrated that he won't communicate with her on a deeper level.

A Self-Test for Stress

If you answer several of the following questions in the affirmative, you may be having some trouble coping with life's stresses and strains.

1. *Why, I oughta . . .* Do you often have angry conversations going on inside your head? Do you have trouble letting go of anger when someone offends you?
2. *Here we go again.* Do you often find yourself anticipating arguments with your co-workers, wife and children, and friends?
3. *What, me worry?* Do you experience feelings of anxiety that you can't connect to a specific circumstance in your life? Do you find yourself often worrying and ruminating about inconsequential events?
4. *Oh, my aching . . .* Do you suffer from physical complaints such as headaches, digestive problems, backaches, neck and shoulder strain?
5. *I left my mind at the office.* Is it difficult for you to get your mind off work-related (and other) responsibilities— even when you have been home for several hours?
6. *I sleep like a baby.* Are you like the stressed-out coach who once told reporters he was sleeping like a baby: "I wake up every half hour and cry."? Do you have trouble getting to sleep and do you wake up often?
7. *I can't believe I ate the whooole thing.* Have you noticed any changes in your eating habits? Do you overeat, eat compulsively, or have you lost your your appetite?
8. *I'll fly away.* Do you often find yourself fantasizing about quitting your job? Moving to an exotic South Pacific island? Taking flight to escape your problems with stress?

Stress Is Epidemic

No one is immune to the pressures and strains of life. Since we can't avoid stress, we've got to find ways to cope with it so that it doesn't ravage our physical and emotional health.

Men who don't learn how to manage stress make themselves vulnerable to a number of mental, emotional, and physical diseases and disorders. The consequences of stress are obvious: anxiety disorders, depression, addictions, compulsions, and anger. Stress can do equally as much damage physically. Scientists tell us stress is a major factor in cardiovascular diseases; it can weaken the immune system; and it may even make us more vulnerable to cancer.

If you're like most American men I know, you can readily identify what is causing stress in your life. What is stressful to one man may not be to another. Only you know what does it for you. But some of the major stressors of contemporary American men include:

Time Pressures

This is the feeling that you're always running behind schedule and you can never accomplish everything you need to get done. You have a gigantic imaginary clock in your head and you constantly hear the obnoxious thing ticking off the seconds, minutes, hours, and days.

Chronic (Unresolved) Problems

These are the ongoing situations in your life that you feel should be resolved but they keep hanging around indefinitely.

Let's say you have a son who keeps getting into trouble at school. You have a conference with his teacher and the principal. Your son is contrite and agrees to change his ways. Then, two days later, you get a call at your office. "Mr. Smith, this is the principal calling. Could you please come to school and take your son home? He's on suspension for beating up another student.''

Most men like to resolve issues and see them stay resolved. This might be possible if you could take the time needed to devote to each issue and get to the bottom of it. However, this is not always possible. A chronic illness or a long-term financial weight, for instance, may take longer to resolve, if ever. Learn to refocus and find joy in the simple pleasures of life. De-stress in little ways (discussed later in this chapter). On the positive side, chronic problems can cause a Christian to develop a greater dependency on the Lord.

Dissatisfaction With One's Spiritual Life

You don't seem to be able to find time to spend alone with God. When you do, you can't get your mind to cooperate. It keeps reminding you of all of the things you have to do. Perhaps you're dissatisfied with your spiritual relationships. Some men are fortunate to be involved with a church that makes an effort to meet their spiritual needs in a fellowship of believers. Other men are frustrated with fellowships that seem to be content to play church rather than *be* the church.

Not Enough Fun, Recreation, and Leisure

Have you ever felt that all of the fun has gone out of your life? Does it seem that your life has become a relentless exercise of meeting the demands and expectations of everyone else (your boss, your wife, your children, your parents)? Have you given up on the idea that life is supposed to be at least somewhat enjoyable? If you have, join the club.

Mini-Vacations:
A Time for Refreshing

You've used up all your vacation time for the year but you need to get away for a few days of fun and relaxation. Your weekends have become routine and predictable. Maybe it's time to get out of the weekend rut you've found yourself in lately and break loose for an enjoyable and revitalizing mini-vacation.

Two- and three-day mini-vacations can provide you with a much-needed respite from the stresses and worries of modern life. It is an opportunity to have a change of scenery, a change of perspective, and probably even a change of clothing (from your office suit to jeans and a T-shirt).

To get away from it all for two or three days, you might want to leave your geographic area. Most of us don't have to travel more than a couple of hundred miles to enjoy a change of scenery.

Here are some other tips you might want to keep in mind when you take your next mini-vacation:

- Save enough money to be able to spend a night or two in a nice motel, cottage, or bed and breakfast. Nothing spoils a weekend getaway more than spending a night in a dumpy or noisy motel.
- While you will likely take the kids along on some of your mini-vacation excursions, consider leaving them with Grandma a time or two. You and your wife need time alone together, away from your parental duties.
- If you can afford it, consider flying to your destination. That way you won't wear yourself out driving. Ask a travel agent in your city to investigate some discount airline rates for you.
- If possible, head for a body of water or to the mountains. Spend a couple of days at the beach watching the waves and the sailboats. Do some fly-fishing in a clear mountain stream. You'll feel like a new man come Monday morning.

- Don't talk about work or home responsibilities while away. Leave those worries for when you get home. You should find that you are in a better frame of mind to handle them after you have gotten away for some rest and recuperation.
- Avoid large population areas and tourist traps as much as possible. Nothing is more discouraging than returning from a mini-vacation more tired and stressed out than you were before you left. You will probably want to save that sight-seeing trip to the Big Apple for your regular two-week-or-more summer vacation.

Last but not least, have a good time and leave your cares and worries behind you. You really do deserve a break!

Being Sandwiched

Many men reading this may be young enough to have small children and old enough to have parents in nursing homes. Not only are you pressured to meet the needs of your wife and children, you may be carrying responsibilities for the well-being of aging parents, as well.

While worrying about how you're going to save enough money to send your kids to college, you may also be wondering how you're going to pay for special home-care treatment of your seventy-eight-year-old mother who has major medical problems.

You may feel overwhelmed with the responsibilities of a demanding job, a wife and family, church commitments, and taking care of your home and vehicles. But how do you find time to provide emotional support and encouragement to an elderly parent—especially one who lives hundreds of miles away? When you've got a mountain of bills on your desk that need to be paid, how do you find the time to see that your elderly parent's financial obligations are all being met?

Marital Difficulties

Even the best of marriages undergo times of strain and stress. There may be communication problems, frequent disagreements over use of money, child-rearing issues, or arguments about division of responsibilities. It's not always easy for two people—who may have had distinctly different life experiences before they were married—to remain in unity and maintain constant harmony in the home.

Unhealthy Habits

This is stress that you may bring upon yourself. Bad habits can stress your body, mind, and spirit. These may include smoking, drinking, poor diet, too much caffeine, lack of proper exercise, and gambling.

———

Now that we've identified some of the top stressors of American males, let's talk about what we can do to better handle them.

Taking Stock of Major Stressors

What sets you off? Sometimes it helps to do an inventory of the major stressors we are forced to cope with while living on this imperfect planet. You can't begin to reduce stress in your life until you identify what has been causing it.

You'll want to take a look at areas such as your job, your home and family life, relationships outside of your family, your spiritual life, your finances, and environmental and health factors.

Life, by nature, is often difficult. For this reason, none of us will ever be able to completely eliminate stress from our lives. But if you inventory your major stressors, you may be able to come up with a plan to help reduce stress and make the problems in your life more manageable.

Jason's personal finances have been causing him stress. He has had to make too many credit card purchases lately, and the interest on the cards is killing his budget. He doesn't know how he is going to be able to keep up with the monthly payments.

The situation has been making Jason feel frustrated and helpless. Since he can't think of a way to increase his income to pay off the credit card debt, Jason has deemed this problem unsolvable.

But after doing an inventory and determining that this financial problem is adding a load of stress to his life, Jason decides to set out to see if there is *something* he can do to lessen it. He calls a friend from his church who is a financial expert and asks for his advice. The friend recommends that he work out a bill consolidation loan with his company's credit union. The credit union offers Jason a low enough rate for the loan that the money he normally has to pay out monthly for the credit card debt is reduced by nearly half!

Voilà! An "unsolvable" problem is solved.

Obviously, not all of the stressful problems in your life can be remedied so easily. But many of life's major stressors can be dealt with successfully if we are willing to identify them and set out to make some changes.

So, what's been bugging you lately?

How Are You Wired?

Mental health experts tell us that stress doesn't necessarily have to be a byproduct of negative circumstances in our lives. But how we are wired to react to those circumstances will go a long way toward determining our stress levels.

John was furious and got a pounding headache after a tree fell on his car. He told himself that this was the most horrible thing that could ever happen to a human being.

The same day in the same city, Steve's wife wrecked his new car. Steve wasn't happy about the situation but chose to take it in stride. Steve told his wife that he was relieved no one was injured.

John's problem caused him major stress because his car was so valuable to him and because he was used to controlling everything in his life. When something happened beyond his control, he became anxious and angry.

Steve talked himself through the situation in a different way. He told himself that his family is more important to him than his car. He recognized that life throws us a curve now and then. The car wreck was simply one of those things we all have to deal with from time to time.

Whether you know it or not, you have a conscious choice to make about how you react to life's shocks and jolts. You can actually rewire your reactions, no matter how you've customarily reacted to stressors in the past.

Psychologists have coined a term to describe how many people cause themselves undue stress and anxiety. Some people catastrophize a difficult situation by letting fear and anger run wild.

Let's say you wake up at nine one morning and find a small lump on the side of your neck. By nine-fifteen you've convinced yourself it's cancer. By ten you're ready to call your lawyer to have him make out your will. Based on what you're telling yourself, you've already turned this discovery into a major catastrophe.

That afternoon you see your doctor and he tells you the lump is a swollen gland. A blood test confirms a viral infection. You've spent most of the day with sweaty hands and a churning stomach, ruminating about how terrible it will be to undergo chemotherapy and surgery.

To handle stress in a way that is healthy and productive, many of us can benefit from learning how to reprogram our stress responses. Here are three steps you can take to react more positively to life's unexpected turns:

1. *When a negative event occurs, don't respond impulsively.* Back away from the situation and give yourself time to think clearly before you respond. You may also want to talk with a friend before you make any decision.

2. *Try to keep the event in perspective by utilizing positive self talk.* While having a tree fall on your car is frustrating, you can remind yourself that you're fortunate to have escaped the mishap uninjured. Plus, insurance will take care of the damage. In a few weeks your car will look like new.

3. *Change your physical response to stressors.* Take a deep breath and hold it to a count of ten before letting it out slowly. Lounge in a recliner for a few minutes. Put on some relaxing music. Close your eyes. Have someone massage your neck and shoulder muscles. Go for a walk.

Managing Your Time

Another important area of learning to handle life's stresses and strains involves how you manage your time.

So many of the men I know who complain the most about stress have overextended themselves in many areas. We often call this tendency "biting off more than you can chew."

I know many stressed-out guys who complain incessantly about being under constant duress because of time limitations. But these are the same folks who—when they have a weekend off—will travel some two hundred miles to attend a Christian family dynamics seminar instead of staying home and having fun with their kids.

Many of these folks (psychologists call them Type-A personalities) find it difficult to just say no. If a pastor asks them to teach a class, they'll do it even though they don't have time to mow the lawn at home. If someone needs to work overtime at the office, they'll be the first to volunteer (even though they don't really need the extra money).

If you're like many working people, you may carry a pocket calendar with you during your workday that helps you keep track of job-related appointments and deadlines. Have you ever thought about scheduling your time away from your workplace?

One man I know keeps a large calendar on his desk at home and pencils in social and recreational times that he wants to set aside during each month of the year. This, he says, is not to give himself more rigid structure in his life but to ensure that he gives himself ample opportunities for fellowship and fun.

Your wife and children want what's best for you, and they want Dad to be healthy and happy. So it's important that you explain to your family that you need time for yourself and time alone with God. Your wife and children can survive without you for a few hours each week. Tell them about your plans ahead of time, and let them know when you've scheduled your recreation and retreat times.

Zeal

Another way to handle stress in your life is to allow yourself to be human—which means you don't beat yourself up when you make mistakes. Perfectionistic people are generally stressed people. It's important that we set high standards for ourselves, but it's just as important that we allow ourselves to sometimes be less than perfect. Many Christian men put themselves in a bind by having unrealistic expectations for their spiritual life, their career, and their family life. Spiritually, they hold themselves responsible for the salvation of every unsaved human being on the planet. Career-wise, they're not satisfied with anything less than being president of the company. At home, they blame themselves if their children aren't straight-A students and all-conference athletes.

God has a plan and a purpose for our lives, and it's a high calling. He wants us to hear His voice and to respond to His leading, but He does not expect perfection from us. There is only one man who has walked among us who is perfect, and that is the Lord Jesus Christ himself. Thank God for the grace that allows me to know and love the Creator of the universe in spite of my glaring imperfections and weaknesses. The blood of Jesus covers my sins. God's grace has indeed set us free!

Since God has given us this freedom, we often make mistakes. Many men don't realize the consequences of ignoring health-sustaining life-style practices when it comes to coping with the stresses and strains of life. When you're healthy, your body can better handle the ravages of stress. When you've been weakened by poor diet, not enough sleep, or not enough exercise, your body is more vulnerable to the health-robbing consequences of stress.

In the chapters about nutrition and supplements, you've learned that stress can deplete your body of certain nutrients that it needs for normal function. You know that a well-balanced diet and supplementation with a vitamin/mineral product will help to compensate for some of the nutrients depleted by stress. But there are other aspects of your life-style that can also either add to your stress load or reduce it.

Environmental Stressors

Perhaps you've never thought much about how chemicals in your home and office may be affecting your body's ability to handle stress and strain. As I mentioned in chapter 4, more than 70,000 new chemicals have been introduced into our society since World War II. According to the California Public Interest Research Group, the U.S. produces a total of 250 billion pounds of synthetic chemicals each year.[1]

Let's take a look at one of these chemicals: Formaldehyde is found in a large number of products we use every day including deodorants, air fresheners, shampoos, mouthwashes, toothpastes, cosmetics, facial tissues, napkins, diaper liners, sheets and other bedding materials, clothing, draperies, carpeting, plywood, paint, wallpaper, and more.

Formaldehyde has been proven to cause cancer in animals. Testing hasn't yet proven it can cause cancer in humans (though many scientists suspect that it can). But professionals in the medical community do know that exposure to formaldehyde can cause such symptoms as headaches, watery eyes, asthma, bronchitis, joint pain, chronic fatigue, disorientation, depression, chest pain, heart palpitations, chronic ear infections, dizziness, and sinusitis.

Yet despite formaldehyde's known toxicity, it is a substance as commonly found in an average American household as butter and milk. And formaldehyde is only *one* of thousands of chemicals we're being exposed to every day of our lives.

Recently we had some carpet installed in the living room of our home. I had been to the library doing some research and came back while the carpet padding was being nailed down. The minute I walked through the open door, I knew something was wrong. My head began pounding, my stomach churned, and my hands began to shake. I walked back out the door and into my backyard, and the symptoms quickly disappeared. The carpet padding contained a toxic chemical that made me extremely ill. So even though most of the padding had been nailed down, we had it pulled up and the carpet installed directly over the wooden floor.

It would be great if you and I could create an environment for ourselves totally devoid of man-made toxic chemicals. But unless we're willing to live like the American pioneers of a hundred and fifty years ago, chemicals are going to be a part of everyday living for all of us. Recognizing this fact, I do all that I can to reduce my exposure to toxic chemicals and to try to create the most health-sustaining environment in my home as is possible. The biggest mistake you and I can make is to believe that a chemical product is safe because it is sold in a store.

Did you know, for example, that the U.S. Food and Drug Administration (FDA) only tests about one percent of the food sold in stores for pesticide residues and that more than half of the pesticides used on food crops can't be detected by routine laboratory methods?[2]

Testing is often conducted by the manufacturer of the product rather than by independent or government researchers. Many manufacturers commonly finance their own testing because the government does not have the man power or the budget to do all of the testing itself.

According to the Center for Science in the Public Interest, dishwashing detergents are responsible for more household poisonings than any other product. But, amazingly, dishwashing detergents are not even regulated by the FDA.[3]

If you are concerned about your health, you probably read nutrition labels on food products to see how much fat and sodium they contain and the number of calories per serving. It is also wise to read labels on household products that you use routinely. Again, it is nearly impossible in this day and age to avoid toxic chemicals completely, but we should do all we can to reduce our exposure to them as much as possible.

Potent man-made chemicals can weaken your immune system, cause fatigue, cause allergic reactions, and render you generally less capable of coping with the pressures of day-to-day living, thus adding to your overall stress load.

Many household products are specially advertised as being all natural, free of toxins, or having no chemicals. Generally these are the best household products to buy. There are also some effective products on the market for spraying on foods to reduce pesticide contamination. These can be purchased through the TV home shopping channels or at some of the large grocery chain stores.

In chapter 4, I discussed how you can take steps to improve the quality of your water. You can also improve the quality of the air you breathe in your home (and even your office) by purchasing an air cleaner. These machines are available at most large discount stores and are reasonably priced. Air cleaners help remove chemicals, cigarette smoke, radon, dust, pollen, mold, bacteria, and viruses from the environment in your home or workplace. They are especially helpful to people who have allergies, asthma, or who are sensitive to chemicals (a medical condition called multiple-chemical sensitivity). Many health experts recommend buying air cleaners that have HEPA filters.

A Good Night's Sleep

Another aspect of your life-style that can affect how well you're able to cope with stress has to do with a normal daily activity that occupies a large chunk of your time: sleep.

Medical scientists say that the sleep needs of each individual varies. Some people function well on six hours of sleep, others need eight or nine hours to feel alert and refreshed.

To get a good night's sleep, it is wise to prepare yourself a few hours in advance of going to bed. Health experts advise against drinking any beverage that contains caffeine after three or four in the afternoon. Give yourself some wind-down time by reducing your activities as bedtime approaches. And because you are going to be in your bedroom for approximately eight hours each night, you should do everything you can to make it as clean and pleasant a place as possible. An air cleaner, for instance, can facilitate easier breathing and make the environment in your bedroom more conducive to sleep.

Men who have problems getting to sleep and staying asleep should consult with their doctor because some sleeping problems are caused by medical conditions. Many large hospitals now have sleep-disorder clinics and specialists who diagnose and treat sleep-related problems.

If you are told by your doctor that your sleep-related problems are not connected to any medical condition, there are some natural remedies available that may help. Two herbs used for this purpose are chamomile and valerian root. Both are sold in capsule form and in tea products.

I have found that when my mind is focused at night on stress-provoking or troubling situations that prevent sleep, it helps to read the Scriptures—especially the Psalms. One of my favorites to read at night is Psalm 4:8: "I will lie down and sleep in peace, for you alone, O Lord, make me dwell in safety."

The last aspect of stress management that I want to cover in this chapter has to do with learning how to relax your body by practicing some simple stress-reducing techniques.

Releasing the Pressure Valve

Let's take a look at a few of the more tried and true relaxation techniques:

Deep-Breathing Exercises

Breathing deeply sends more oxygen to the cells, invigorating you and bringing about relaxation simultaneously. I take a deep breath, hold it in for ten seconds, and let it out slowly. When I feel myself becoming especially stressed, breathing deeply can almost instantly make me feel more relaxed and in control.

Progressive Muscle Relaxation

When a person is under stress, his muscles become tense. Progressive muscle relaxation uses your thinking processes to cause the muscles to relax. It isn't mysticism or hocus-pocus but simply using your brain to tell your muscles what to do.

You begin by tensing and untensing your extremities—usually starting with the feet and moving up through all parts of the body. Most people report feeling much more relaxed and calm afterward.

If you are interested in learning more about progressive muscle relaxation, contact your local mental health organization for information about classes and seminars that teach this technique. Your local library may also have information in the health or mental-health sections.

Spiritual (Christian) Meditation

If you think meditation is only practiced by Eastern mystics and New Agers, consult your Bible concordance. Consider Psalm 119:27: "Let me understand the teaching of your precepts; then I will meditate on your wonders."

The gurus of Yoga teach their adherents to quiet themselves by repeating mantras that are often only sounds such as "Oooommmmm." This is *not* what I'm talking about when I speak of Christian meditation.

Find a place of peace and quiet. Close your eyes to shut out any distractions. Pray, asking God to be present with you. Choose a verse or portion of Scripture or an attribute of God on which to focus your thoughts. Christian meditation accomplishes two things: It calms you, allowing your mind and body to rest and be at peace. It helps you to zero in on eternal truths and to connect with God without outside distractions or influences.

I often focus on some aspect of God's nature (such as His mercy) and ponder evidences of His mercy that I've experienced personally or read about in the Word. My mind is in a somewhat passive state. I let unwanted thoughts pass by without consciously trying to get rid of them. My times of Christian meditation are relatively short, between fifteen and thirty minutes, but I always feel physically and spiritually revived after a brief time of meditation and reflection.

We've covered a number of aspects of reducing and managing stress in our lives in this chapter. Perhaps there are other methods you utilize in your own life to help you cope with stresses and strains. Ultimately, a lasting solution can be found by simply turning your worries and fears over to God, admitting to Him that you can't handle all that the world throws at you. In 1 Peter 5:7, we read, "Cast all your anxiety on him because He cares for you."

For Thought and Discussion

1. How much stress do you have in your life? What circumstances in your life are particularly stressful to you?
2. How do you handle stress? What do you do to cope with daily pressures?
3. Can you identify aspects of your life-style and home environment that may be adding to your "stress load" and diminishing your body's ability to cope with the effects of stress?
4. Do you add stress and pressure to your life by having unrealistic expectations? Do you have a perfectionistic attitude?

Notes

1. Nancy Sokol Green, *Poisoning Our Children: Surviving in a Toxic World* (Chicago: The Noble Press, Inc., 1991), 14.
2. Ibid., 47.
3. Ibid., 89.

The Rubber Meets the Road

Today—in fact, at this very moment—you can decide to begin making some changes in your life that will set you on the road to better physical, emotional, and spiritual health and well-being.

We've covered a lot of ground, and hopefully you've learned a lot about taking care of yourself. Perhaps you've already started making some changes in your life-style. I hope so. Maybe you're waiting until you've finished the last page of this book before you begin to map out your personal strategy.

Whatever the case, don't let anything divert your attention or distract you from achieving your goals. This is too important to put off for another day. Why not start now?

Let's check on the stories of some of the men from the first chapter. They've pursued their health goals with some great results.

Stan

Stan is the guy who worked fifteen-hour days at his law office and then found himself facing a night in a hospital.

Stan was fortunate. An emergency room doctor examined him and told him that he was simply reacting to severe stress. The shortness of breath and pressure in his chest were both stress related. The pain in his arm turned out to be a pinched nerve from a church league softball game.

But Stan took this episode as a warning that he needed to make some adjustments in his life. He began to be more careful about his diet, cutting down on fast-food meals and fats and eating more vegetables, grains, and fruits. He also decided to reduce his workweek to fifty hours from seventy-five, and began the healthy habit of taking a brisk walk each evening before supper.

Tony

After taking inventory of his life and evaluating the direction he was headed, Tony knew a major crisis was in his future if he didn't make some changes. He'd heard of a Christian men's support group in a nearby community and decided to check it out.

At first he was afraid the men in the group would judge him because he often drank as a way to escape his problems. But he found to his surprise that others in the group had also had problems with drinking and substance abuse. These men accepted him with open arms and committed themselves to supporting him.

Some members told Tony to feel free to contact one of them if he felt tempted to drink his way out again. They promised encouragement if he would agree to be held spiritually accountable to them.

At last Tony found what had been missing from his life. His drinking episodes became less frequent until he came to the place where he no longer needed to numb himself with alcohol. With God's help—and the help of his newfound Christian brothers—he faces each new day with hope and confidence.

Roger

Roger and his wife went to a Christian marriage counselor because Roger was at the end of his rope. He was tired of being smothered by his wife's constant demands for all of his time and attention.

Roger knew that his wife's parents had divorced when she was a young child, but he hadn't understood all the ramifications until the counselor brought them to the surface. His wife's father had left the family and moved to another state, causing her to live with a constant fear of being abandoned by a man—this time, by her husband.

Roger assured her that he would never abandon her as her father had but that he needed some freedom and some time to himself.

With the help of the counselor, Roger and his wife worked out an agreement by which Roger was given the better part of one day a week to himself with no family responsibilities.

Roger began using his "time off" to take long walks in the park, to peruse shopping centers, attend sports events with friends, and find some quiet time to pray and connect with his heavenly Father.

Since then Roger's emotional outlook has improved as well as his physical health. His wife has benefited from her husband's newfound liberation, as well: she has learned to handle more responsibilities on her own and to depend less on her husband. And she is pleased that she has been able to contribute to Roger's improved emotional and physical health.

John

John called a meeting of his elder board and told them that he was concerned about his physical and emotional health because church-related responsibilities were overwhelming him.

The church had been collecting funds for a new building addition, but John asked that the money be used to hire an additional pastoral staff member. The elders, recognizing the certain danger of burnout in their pastor, agreed to John's proposal.

When the new assistant pastor arrived, John shook the man's hand and told him he would see him again in about three weeks. John and his wife were headed to Hawaii for a long-overdue honeymoon. Because of church duties, they'd never been able to have a real honeymoon.

After he returned from his trip, John planned to make further adjustments to lessen his workload by delegating more responsibility to other staff members and layleaders.

God Gives Second Chances

Not long ago my preschool-age son and I were alone in the living room of my mother's home. Seeing my son constructively occupied with crayons and a coloring book, I drifted off to sleep.

Suddenly, in a half-awake stupor, I heard a clipping sound and felt something feathery fall on my neck. To my shock and dismay, I discovered my son had given me a trim with his grandmother's scissors!

"Lincoln, I can't believe you cut Daddy's hair!" I yelled. His expression changed from a bemused grin to a frown, realizing he had incurred his dad's wrath. While I went to the bathroom to survey the damage, my boy went in the opposite direction—the corner of my mother's kitchen.

When I came out, ready to deal with his misbehavior, I heard a small, solemn voice: "Dear God," my son prayed, his eyes tightly closed and his lips pursed. "I'm so sorry I cut my daddy's hair and did something bad to make you sad. Please forgive me, God."

My anger faded and tears welled up in my eyes. I was witnessing the Holy Spirit's work in my son's heart, and it was a very moving moment for me.

Needless to say, Lincoln received no punishment for his misdeed. Rather, he got a second chance from his dad and learned something, as well: he's never tried to play barber since.

You have the opportunity to begin to make some changes in your life that will result in better health and greater happiness for you in the years to come. Your Father in heaven may be giving you a second chance that could change your life.

What Have We Learned?

Let's summarize some of the areas we've covered. This may help you to formulate your own personal plan for making health-promoting changes in your life.

Nutrition

We discussed how the "Standard American Diet" has robbed many people of their health but also warned against dietary legalism, which can be counterproductive.

We learned that a healthy diet should be one high in fiber, high in complex carbohydrates, and low in fats and sugars—with an emphasis on eating lots of vegetables, fruits, and grains. We also took a look at how important it is to make certain that your drinking water is pure.

Exercise

Boredom is the main obstacle to stand in the way of a man being consistent with an exercise program. We suggested ways to make exercise more enjoyable and how to get good aerobic value from your efforts. We also explored ways to get extra exercise during a busy workday.

Supplements

We learned that taking vitamin, mineral, and other dietary supplements is becoming a necessity in this era of fast-food meals, stress, and environmental toxins.

Popular herbal and hormonal products were examined, and we warned against quick-fix supplements that don't deliver on their promises. We were reminded how to avoid overdosing on supplements and how to take them more safely and with the best therapeutic benefit.

Coping With Stress

Mental, emotional, and physical consequences of stress were evaluated, and we talked about some of the major stressors for contemporary men. We took a look at time pressures, chronic (unresolved) problems, marital strains, dissatisfaction with one's spiritual life, and other factors that contribute to our stress loads. We also discussed how to make our homes and offices more health-sustaining and learned some simple stress-reducing techniques.

Other Topics

We've covered a broad range of issues relating to emotional and spiritual well-being. Some of these include:

- Identifying wounds from the past and letting the Father heal them,
- Spending quality time alone with God,
- Developing healthy relationships that meet our needs for support and emotional and spiritual intimacy,
- Confronting barriers that prevent us from meeting our health-maintenance goals.

Your Behavioral Contract

Now it's time for you to begin to make a behavioral contract with yourself based upon what you have learned. You will want to inventory such areas in your life as your eating habits, sleeping habits, exercise, your spiritual and social life, and how you handle stress.

Every man is an individual. No two behavioral contracts will look alike. But to help you develop a contract, let's take a look at how one man formulated his and put it into practice.

Brad's Nutrition Contract

Brad decided to limit his consumption of animal fats to fish and chicken. He began to eat more multi-grain foods, vegetables, and fruits, and added olive oil to his salads. Brad began to reduce his sugar intake to an occasional piece of pie or a couple of cookies. He ate less at each meal but began to eat smaller meals more frequently.

Wanting some nutritional "insurance," Brad found a good multi-vitamin and mineral supplement at a local health-food store and began taking it every day. Because his doctor said he had borderline high cholesterol, he also began taking garlic capsules. In the winter months, he bought some echinacea capsules to reduce his chances of getting a cold or flu.

Brad's Exercise Contract

Brad decided that walking would be the most suitable form of exercise for his life-style. He began walking a mile a day with a goal to extend that distance by one mile every other month. He bought a pair of weights to exercise his arms and shoulder muscles and a ski machine to use when he couldn't get outside to walk because of bad weather.

Brad found a parking garage about a half-mile from his office and began parking his car there so that he could enjoy a brisk walk two or three times during every workday.

Brad's Stress-Reduction Contract

Though he wasn't in a position to leave his stressful job and find a new one, Brad evaluated his work life and decided to make some adjustments. He began to delegate more duties to lower-level management, take a lunch break in the middle of the day (instead of eating at his desk), and leave his office no later than five-thirty.

Brad and his wife consulted a Christian marriage counselor and began to learn how to improve their communication. Brad also checked out some library books to learn relaxation techniques and began practicing them daily.

In taking inventory of his mental outlook, Brad realized he had become too perfectionistic—expecting perfection from himself, his wife, and other family members. With this insight, Brad began to give himself more slack to be less than perfect. He also lowered unreasonable expectations he had for his wife and children. Brad now sets aside time each day to be alone with God, and he is enjoying the intimate fellowship he is now having with his heavenly Father.

Brad's Relationship Contract

Realizing that he had no friends outside of his co-workers at the office, Brad determined to get to know some of the men at his church. He joined a Saturday night men's fellowship group and began attending cell group meetings on Tuesday nights. Brad is learning how to become more open, honest, and vulnerable in his relationships with other Christians.

Stay in the Game

Brad used some of the information in this book to begin making changes that will make him a healthier and happier man. My fervent hope and prayer is that you will do the same by developing your personal behavioral contract. I also hope that you'll develop an evangelical attitude toward health-related issues—that you will go out and share some of this information with other men. They really do need to hear it!

Have you ever seen an athlete who has sustained an injury in a game standing on the sidelines watching his teammates play? If you catch a close-up of his face, you'll notice he looks frustrated and disappointed because he can no longer make a contribution to the game. Too many Christians are on the sidelines, knocked out of the game of life early due to physical or emotional health problems that could have been prevented.

Use It or Lose It

Taking care of one's health is a lot like taking care of an automobile. I had a friend whose parents bought him a car when he was in college. He knew nothing about car maintenance, and apparently no one taught him when they gave him the keys. He drove the car for many months without changing the oil, and it eventually ended up in a junkyard with a blown engine. Had my friend changed the oil regularly and had other maintenance work done on a regular basis, he would have had a dependable car to drive for many years to come.

Like a car, our bodies and minds need to be maintained to function properly. To neglect any area of health maintenance is as unwise as driving a car without changing the oil. The difference is you can always buy another car, but you've only been given one body to last a lifetime, so you need to take good care of it.

I don't believe it is God's plan for your life that you end up in the proverbial junkyard at age forty, fifty, or sixty. His plan is that you enjoy a long life (Psalm 91:15–16); that you be as blessed as David was when he wrote, "Surely goodness and love will follow me all the days of my life" (Psalm 23:6).

Your health is a valuable and precious commodity. Be good to yourself. *Now* is the time to start taking better care of your body, mind, and spirit!

For Thought and Discussion

1. What have you learned from this book that will help you to improve your life-style?
2. What areas of your life need the most improvement?
3. What changes do you plan to make? What is your plan of action?
4. What do you hope these changes will accomplish in your life?

Thank you for selecting a book from
BETHANY HOUSE PUBLISHERS

Bethany House Publishers is a ministry of Bethany Fellowship International, an interdenominational, nonprofit organization committed to spreading the Good News of Jesus Christ around the world through evangelism, church planting, literature distribution, and care for those in need. Missionary training is offered through Bethany College of Missions.

Bethany Fellowship International is a member of the National Association of Evangelicals and subscribes to its statement of faith. If you would like further information, please contact:

Bethany Fellowship International
6820 Auto Club Road
Minneapolis, MN 55438 USA